Dreams and Thunder

Dreams and Thunder

Stories, Poems, and
The Sun Dance Opera

Zitkala-Ša

Edited by P. Jane Hafen

UNIVERSITY OF NEBRASKA PRESS
LINCOLN AND LONDON

Library of Congress
Cataloging-in-Publication Data
Zitkala-Ša, 1876–1938.
Dreams and Thunder:
stories, poems, and
The sun dance opera / Zitkala-Ša;
edited by P. Jane Hafen
p.   cm.
Includes bibliographical
references (p.   )
ISBN 0-8032-4918-7
(cloth: alk. paper)
1. Indians of North America
—Literary collections.
2. Indians of North America
—Folklore.
I. Hafen, P. Jane, 1955–
II. Title
PS3549.I89 D74 2001

"N"

Contents

Illustrations

Acknowledgments

I first encountered the works of Zitkala-Ša (Gertrude Simmons Bonnin) while working on a master's thesis at Brigham Young University in the early 1980s.[1] I discovered *The Sun Dance Opera* while searching for Indian stereotypes in the work of Mormon artists. Although William F. Hanson refers to Bonnin as a "Mormon convert," I was unable to verify that claim. I was puzzled that a Sioux woman would be caught up in what appeared to be a parody of sacred ritual. I made a mental note to follow up on the work of Zitkala-Ša.

My opportunity to pursue the enigma of Zitkala-Ša did not come until 1993, when I received a Frances C. Allen Fellowship to study at the D'Arcy McNickle Center for the History of the American Indian at the Newberry Library in Chicago. Under the direction of Fred Hoxie, I researched primary documents, including the *American Indian Magazine* editorials, Society of American Indians documents, and Bonnin's correspondence with John Collier on microfilm. Ironically, my search led back to BYU.

As a former BYU professor, William Hanson willed his documents to the university's archive collection. These documents included information, clippings, and reminiscences about Zitkala-Ša and *The Sun Dance Opera*. Much to my surprise, the BYU archive collections also contained many boxes of documents in a Bonnin collection and Bonnin-related materials in the papers of Ernest L. Wilkinson. The Bonnin documents at BYU included the previously unpublished stories, speeches, and diary excerpts.[2] Where possible, I have noted the dates and Gertrude's own comments, but most of the typed manuscripts are not dated. I have tried to leave the manuscripts close to the way Zitkala-Ša did, but spelling has been corrected and punctuation has been silently added for clarity. Much of Zitkala-Ša's writing reveals that she spoke English as a second language. Some compound words and hyphenated adjectives are split, and some verbs reflect Biblical rhetoric. Her usage also reflects the language of her time. She was inconsistent with some spellings and capitalization.

In 1938 John Collier, commissioner of Indian affairs, issued an executive order that only lawyers could represent claims before the Indian Land Claims Commission. Although Raymond Bonnin, Gertrude's husband, was employed by the Uintah Ouray Utes and had studied law, he had not been admitted to the bar. He entered an agreement with Wilkinson's law firm, who would formally represent the Utah tribe. Raymond later sold most of his interest in any future settlement to Wilkinson. Raymond died in 1942, like Gertrude, intestate. When the Ute claims were finally settled in 1951, Wilkinson administered Bonnin's financial share to the grandchildren. The same year the Bonnin documents were forwarded from a Virginia probate lawyer, James Simmonds, to BYU, where Wilkinson was president.

Additional sources for this collection include the following: publications from *The Earlhamite*, Earlham College, Indiana; The Carlos Montezuma Papers, State Historical Society of Wisconsin; Papers of the Society of American Indians (on microfilm at UNLV); documents of the Bureau of Catholic Indian Missions, Marquette University, Milwaukee, Wisconsin; National Archives, Rocky Mountain Depository; John Collier documents; and documents of the Indian Rights Association.

I gratefully acknowledge the estate of Gertrude Bonnin for permission to publish these works. David Whittaker, the late Dennis Rowley, Brad Westwood, Kelly Bullock, and Ellen Copley, archive librarians and staff at BYU, have been most helpful. This work would not be possible without the generous cooperation of Brigham Young University. The English Department, College of Liberal Arts, and University Grants and Fellowships at the University of Nevada, Las Vegas, have been generous in support with research opportunities and technical assistance. I am also grateful for Doreen Rappaport and her willingness to give suggestions and share information. Patrice Hollrah, Suzanne Bergfalk, Venicia Considine, and Janice McIntire-Strasburg assisted with the manuscripts. Janice A. Faulconer and Rebecca A. Roberts helped sort through the uncataloged boxes in the BYU archives. Gwen Griffin, collaborator and friend, offered priceless guidance. My devoted husband, Jeff, helped transcribe *The Sun Dance Opera*.

As I have studied the life and writings of Gertrude Bonnin, I found a spirited and determined woman. She was driven by her passion for justice and her commitment to her Yankton background. The choices she made reflect the paradoxes we American Indians continue to face. She clung to her traditional beliefs while practicing Catholicism and other versions of Christianity; she had a Mormon funeral in Arlington, Virginia. She was wrenched from her traditions by the assimilating boarding school experience, yet she sent her only child to a Catholic school in Nauvoo, Illinois. She performed in public arenas and pandered to sentimental, colonial images while demanding legal rights and national sovereignties for Indians. She resisted Col. Richard H. Pratt's model of assimilation but joined with him in the campaign against legalized peyote use and in advocating the power of education.

Bonnin chose survival, even at the price of melodrama, and mainstream education and religion. Amazingly, she never forgot the essence of her self while demanding the freedom to act within her changing environment: "Give [the first Americans] freedom to do their own thinking; to exercise their judgement; to hold open forums for the expression of their thought, and finally permit them to manage their own personal business" (*Americanize the First American*).

Introduction

Gertrude Simmons Bonnin (1876–1938), also known as Zitkala-Ša, is best known for *American Indian Stories* (1921), a compilation of previously published articles, and *Old Indian Legends* (1901). Her writings have joined the expanding canon of American literature and are represented in numerous anthologies and as objects of postcolonial criticisms.[1] Zitkala-Ša's own accounts of her life are compelling and are among the first Native American autobiographies not filtered through a translator or editor. Her writings possess a distinctive literary style and perspective that reach beyond previously published ethnic autobiographies and traditional storytelling. Fully appreciating Gertrude Bonnin's extraordinary life and powerful voice through her few published writings is difficult, however. Her accomplishments were extensive and include public speaking, editorial writing, political activism, and co-composition of an opera.

Bonnin reflects the multiple cultural influences of her era: a Yankton Sioux upbringing, education in Christian boarding schools, the opportunities of the "New Woman," and growing American Indian activism during the 1920s and the Roosevelt years with John Collier at the helm of the Bureau of Indian Affairs.

Gertrude Bonnin was born on the Yankton Sioux Reservation in 1876, the same year as the Battle of the Greasy Grass (Little Big Horn). Known as Gertrude Simmons, she was the daughter of a white trader named Felker and Ellen Simmons, whose Yankton-Nakota name was Táte I Yóhin Win (Reaches for the Wind).[2]

Bonnin's life traverses the breadth of Sioux language and society. Agnes M. Picotte (Lakota) observes in the foreword to *Old Indian Legends* that Bonnin's Yankton upbringing probably meant that she learned the Nakota dialect of the Siouan language. Her authorial name, Zitkala-Ša, is Lakota. Her Native-language writings are in the third Siouan dialect, Dakota, likely because of the influence of Stephen Return Riggs's early Dakota dictionary and orthographics for the spoken Siouan language or because the Yankton groups also spoke Dakota.[3]

Beatrice Medicine (Lakota) and Vine Deloria Jr. (Dakota) refer to the Yanktons as Dakotas (Ruoff 110 n.56; V. Deloria 7). Karen D. Lone Hill (Oglala Lakota) offers instead the following classification: the Sioux Nation has seven major council divisions, which are the eastern Dakotas (Mdewakantonwan, Wahpekute, Wahpetonwan and Sisitonwan); the Nakota with the southwest Ihanktonwan (Campers of the End, Yankton) and Ihanktonwanna (Little Campers at the End, Yanktonai); and the western Lakotas, or Tetons, comprised of seven bands (Sicangu, Oohenunpa, Itazipacola, Miniconjou, Sihaspa, Hunkpapa and Oglala). Because *Nakota* is more often used as a linguistic classification, the general designation *Yanktons* will be used here (see Bettelyoun and Waggoner 119). Pre-reservation Yanktons and Yanktonais traversed the Yankton triangle from the pipestone quarries at the headwaters of the Des Moines River to the convergence of the Big Sioux River and the Missouri River, heading up the Missouri River. In accordance with the 1858 treaty, the Yankton Reservation was established in 1859, with its agency headquarters at Greenwood, South Dakota (Hoover 29, 40).

Although Plains Indians in the nineteenth century experienced dramatic cultural upheaval, wars, disease, and displacement, Zitkala-Ša tells only of her early, innocent life on the prairies, yet she includes her mother's disillusion with the "palefaces." With little documentary evidence, the reader must depend on Zitkala-Ša's own representations for her early biography: "I was a wild little girl of seven. Loosely clad in a slip of brown buckskin, and lightfooted with a pair of soft moccasins on my feet, I was as free as the wind that blew my hair, and no less spirited than a bounding deer" (*American Indian Stories* 8). She recounts details of tribal life, learning survival skills, and proper behaviors modeled after her mother's actions. Bonnin also learned from oral traditions and became familiar with stories she would later recount. Any tensions from her mixed-blood heritage are not acknowledged in her remembrances. Upon entering the non-Indian world, she was objectified and treated like a full-blood, and she allowed herself to be represented as such.

At the age of eight Bonnin was enticed by missionaries and her friend, Judewin, to the land of "red, red apples" on the "iron horse" (*American Indian Stories* 41–42). Once she arrived at the White's Manual Labor Institute in Wabash, Indiana, she was subjected to the assimilative practices common at most Indian boarding schools of the later nineteenth century. School officials, determined to "civilize" the "savages," introduced her to Christianity, forbade her to speak her language, set her on a schedule of manual labor, and cut her long hair. Of that final humiliation she says, "I cried aloud, shaking my head all the while until I felt the cold blades of the scissors against my neck, and heard them gnaw off one of my thick braids. Then I lost my spirit. Since the day I was taken from my mother I had suffered extreme indignities. People had stared at me. I had been tossed about in the air like a wooden puppet. And now my long hair was shingled like a coward's! In my anguish I moaned for my mother, but no one came to comfort me" (*American Indian Stories* 55–56).

Bonnin's individuality prevailed through minor acts of rebellion. She sabotaged a pot of turnips and scribbled out the devil's eyes in a Bible storybook. She also learned to read and write English. At the same time she was deprived of rites of passage for Sioux young women, she was being socialized into a world alien to her mother and her brother. When visits home became unpleasant, she returned to school: the Santee Agency

School (1889–90), White's Manual Labor Institute (1891–95), and Earlham College in Indiana (1895–97).

At Earlham, she became a showpiece Indian, developing prizewinning skills as an orator, a violinist, a pianist, and a singer. Bonnin became a prime example of the benefits of Indian boarding school education. Even as her teachers took pride in their success, surely she must have appreciated the public validation of her life and abilities that her own mother rejected. She concurrently developed a strong sense of indignation toward racial prejudice and the exploitative system she experienced. Racism did not distinguish mixed from full blood.

In 1896 she participated in an Indiana state oratorical contest and won second place. The experience "left little taste of victory," however, as she was ridiculed publicly. She recalls, "There, before that vast ocean of eyes, some college rowdies threw out a large white flag, with a drawing of a most forlorn Indian girl on it. Under this they had printed in bold black letters words that ridiculed the college which was represented by a 'squaw'" (*American Indian Stories* 79). Ironically, the speech itself, titled "Side by Side," was a stinging indictment of white society and hypocritical Christianity. Reprinted in both the school paper, *The Earlhamite*, and the Santee Agency school paper, *The Word Carrier*, her rhetoric is couched in Biblical language:

> To-day the Indian is pressed almost to the farther sea. Does that sea symbolize his death? Does the narrow territory still left to him typify the last brief day before his place on Earth "shall know him no more forever?" Shall might make right and the fittest alone survive? Oh Love of God and of His "Strong Son," thou who liftest up the oppressed and succorest the needy, is thine ear grown heavy that it cannot hear his cry? Is thy arm so shortened, it cannot save? Dost thou not yet enfold him in thy love? Look with compassion down, and with thine almighty power move this nation to the rescue of my race.

This speech brought Bonnin public acclaim and attention. An unidentified illness prevented her from finishing her degree at Earlham, but she soon began teaching at Carlisle Industrial Training School, working there from 1897 to 1899. She had bitter disagreements with Carlisle founder Col. Richard H. Pratt, and in 1900 she left Pennsylvania to attend the New England Conservatory of Music. She also began publishing articles in the *Atlantic Monthly* (1900, 1902), *Harper's Magazine* (1901), and *Everybody's Magazine* (1902). These works were collected and published as *American Indian Stories* (1921). The articles, particularly the essay titled "Why I Am a Pagan" ("The Great Spirit"), revealed divergences between Pratt's policy of total assimilation and Bonnin's Native pride. She also compiled a collection of Sioux myths, *Old Indian Legends*. This volume of stories steeped in Sioux oral tradition was illustrated by fellow Carlisle teacher Angel De Cora (Winnebago). The traditional stories helped to validate Bonnin's Yankton heritage. She declares in the preface: "The old legends of America belong quite as much to the blue-eyed little patriot as to the black-haired aborigine. And when they are grown tall like the wise grown-ups may they not lack interest in a further study of Indian folklore, a study which so strongly suggests our near kinship with the rest of humanity and points a steady finger toward the great brotherhood of mankind, and by which one is so forcibly impressed with the possible earnestness of life as seen through the teepee door!" (vi).

These public writings appeared under Bonnin's self-given Lakota name, Zitkala-Ša, which means "Red Bird."[4] The name affirmed her sense of Indian identity. She explained to Carlos Montezuma that her mother became disaffected with her father, Felker: "So as I grew I was called by my brother's name—Simmons. I bore it a long time till my brother's wife—angry with me because I insisted upon getting an education said I had deserted home and I might give up my brother's name 'Simmons' too. Well—you can guess how queer I felt away from my own people—home-less—penniless—and even without a name! Then, I chose to make a name for myself—& I guess I have made 'Zitkala-Ša' Known—for even Italy writes it in her language!" (c. June–July 1901).

Carlos Montezuma was a famed Apache doctor and, later, an organizer in pan-Indian movements and national Indian politics. In all likelihood Bonnin met Montezuma at Carlisle when she was teaching there. They became engaged, but Bonnin's commitment to tribal connections led her to return to the Yanktons and ultimately, in 1902, to break off her engagement to Montezuma, who would not leave his medical practice in Chicago. She remained to gather more stories in South Dakota, where in 1902 she married Raymond Telephause Bonnin, also Yankton.

During her engagement to Carlos Montezuma, Bonnin wrote letters to him almost daily. The self-revelations of these letters chart the growing distance between them and their methods of connecting to their Indian identities. Although Montezuma's letters are not available, their contents can be deduced from Bonnin's responses. Almost nine years after her marriage to Raymond Bonnin, she reestablished contact with Montezuma. Her initial approach was conciliatory. Subsequent correspondence between them centered on the Society of American Indians and other political issues. The tone of the letters was courteous and professional.

The Indian Service assigned the Bonnins to the Uintah Ouray Ute Agency in Duchesne, Utah, where they lived from 1902 until 1916. Their only child, Raymond Ohiya, was born in 1903. Gertrude Bonnin taught, clerked, did public speaking, and performed community service under the auspices of the Society of American Indians (SAI) after its organization in 1911. While in Utah, she continued to write stories. Although these stories are generally undated, the typescripts appear prepared for publication submission. The stories continue the themes and tales Bonnin told in her other works: traditional legends and origin stories and tales of whites perpetrating injustices against Indians. No documentation survives to suggest why she did not publish these works.

Bonnin also regularly corresponded with the Bureau of Catholic Indian Missions during her Utah stay. Although much of the correspondence dealt with her financial and logistical circumstances, she also described her experiences with the Uintah Ouray Utes. Her concern for the Christian spiritual welfare of the Utes seems to contradict her pagan manifesto of earlier years. Indeed, her distress over spiritual circumstances led her to ask the Catholic fathers to recommend a Christian boarding school for son Raymond Ohiya.[5]

In 1908, Gertrude and Raymond met and befriended in rural Utah a young music teacher, William F. Hanson (Hanson 74). Drawing upon common musical interests and Wild West shows, Indian cultural performances at fairs, and the tradition of Mormon pageants, Bonnin and Hanson decided to compose an opera with an Indian theme. First they considered the life of Chipeta, widow of Ute leader Ouray, but after seeing the Utes' Sun Dance in the summer of 1910, they settled on that topic.

The Sun Dance Opera is not without controversy. Further complicating the appropriateness of a staged performance of sacred ritual are questions about Hanson's role, which expanded during a revival of the opera in 1938, and the extent of Bonnin's familiarity with the Sun Dance itself. Of all the groups in the Sioux Nation, the Yanktons did not practice the Sun Dance with the same intensity as did the Lakotas (V. Deloria 204). Although both composers asserted the Sioux (their own lack of cultural distinction between Dakotas and Lakotas) roots of the opera in the melodies used for arias, in the use of a wedding flute Raymond Bonnin had given his wife, and in its basic theme, its tribal expression occurred more outside of the written script. The cast of the opera was comprised of classically trained musicians for the primary roles and local Natives for the chorus. At various and crucial times the opera would stop for performances of traditional Native songs and dances. These dances in the original Utah performances were led by a Sioux centenarian—"Old Sioux," or "Bad Hand"—who lived with the Bonnins.

The Sun Dance Opera reveals the sometimes turbulent cultural waters that Bonnin navigated in her life. Often she seemed caught between validating her indigenous beliefs and seeking public approval. Such a position was not necessarily oppositional—as often represented in critical assessments—but part of the complex mediation that Native peoples frequently reconcile in order to survive in the modern era. In the next phase of Bonnin's life, she seemed to become even further removed from her tribal origins; her public role, however, became more entrenched in an aboriginal persona as she worked tirelessly "for the Indian cause."[6]

Also during her Utah experience Bonnin witnessed firsthand the growing peyote culture and rise of the Native American Church. Ironically, she and her former adversary, Colonel Pratt, later united to oppose the use of peyote.

One consequence of Bonnin's reestablishing ties to Carlos Montezuma in 1913 was her involvement in the Society of American Indians, a political pan-Indian group Montezuma had helped found in 1911. She did fieldwork for the society, teaching homemaking skills to the Utes. In 1916, she was elected secretary to the SAI and the Bonnins moved to Washington DC.

Bonnin actively campaigned against peyote in Washington DC, developing skills and connections as a lobbyist that would serve her the rest of her life. She edited the SAI publication *American Indian Magazine* from 1918 through 1919 after SAI president Arthur Parker was ousted from office and defaulted his position as editor. Bonnin contributed editorials that condemned peyote and advocated reform that would recognize World War I Indian soldiers and grant U.S. citizenship for Indians. Some of these editorials also appeared in the *Indian Sentinel*, a publication of the Bureau of Catholic Indian Missions.

Factionalism, intertribal rivalries, and personal conflicts—particularly with Marie Baldwin (Chippewa), another prominent member of the SAI—led Bonnin to leave her position with the SAI in 1919. Raymond Bonnin, who had earned the rank of army captain during World War I, pursued law studies. Together, the Bonnins continued their campaign for Indian citizenship and justice. In 1921, Gertrude Bonnin worked with the General Federation of Women's Clubs to form an Indian Welfare Committee. She wrote a policy brochure, *Americanize the First American: A Plan of Regeneration,* which includes a large circular chart comparing bureaucracy with democracy. She also worked with the Indian Rights Association and the American Indian Defense Association (AIDA), coauthoring a report of abuses entitled *Oklahoma's Poor Rich Indians* (1924).

After Congress granted citizenship to American Indians in 1924, the Bonnins continued their association with Pan-Indian organizations. In 1926 they formed the National Council of American Indians (NCAI) with Bonnin as president and Raymond as secretary. They argued that of the various Pan-Indian groups only the NCAI could claim Indians as executive officers (the Bonnins kept their positions until her death). The Bonnins also helped establish local chapters of the NCAI on numerous reservations. They lobbied Congress and the Bureau of Indian Affairs for individual land and financial claims. The NCAI attempted to establish political power through voting blocs, incorporating an Indian rights plank in the 1928 Republican platform and supporting Democrats in 1932.

Although the NCAI shared offices with the AIDA until 1932, it never benefited from the financial support of other Indian rights organizations. Most of its money came from Gertrude Bonnin's speaking engagements, unsubstantial royalties from her books, and her husband's law work. The Bonnins established a pattern of summer travel to reservations and winters in Washington DC, answering volumes of correspondence and preserving political contacts. Their letters were cordial, yet perfunctory, addressing the logistics of the NCAI.

The passage of the Wheeler Howard/Indian Reorganization Act of 1934 and the appointment of John Collier as commissioner of Indian affairs prompted the Bonnins to rededicate themselves to helping American Indians across the nation. In 1935 they embarked on a road trip to encourage active participation by tribes in organizing their own governing structures. When the Bonnins returned to the Yanktons, with whom they maintained close ties, they were disappointed by the response to their experience and suggestions. They argued strongly for an independent agency, but the Bonnins failed, partly because of ideological differences with John Collier and partly because of tribal factionalism. In a diary, Gertrude Bonnin described this difficult, exhausting, and often emotionally tumultuous effort:

> Discussion of the WHA was the main subject. Bureau employed men under the direction of Supt Robert, is driving night & day in car & gas [is] Govt furnished—crowding the Inds. to accept the Charter & byLaws drawn up by the Bureau. Employees, not lawyers, got up before assembled Inds & grossly misconstrued the WH act. The meeting yesterday agreed to get the aid of high class lawyers to explain the law. & to advise them in protecting themselves & whether it can accept part if not *all* of the WH act?
>
> On our return, thru Greenwood we met Mr. Cleaver. He & his wife and Miss Last of the Mohicans, now employed as Social Service Employees came & stayed & stayed—claiming they wanted to hear our view of this Act etc. R[aymond] expounded the law & its ramifications, eating the very vitals out of the future. . . . All left in friendly spirit—each with mental reservation of the other's opinions in the disturbing WH Act. (August 16, 1935)

Bonnin lamented the lack of response from her fellow Yanktons: "I mentioned [that] I too [was] a little reinvested in [the] tribe thru my work & now I am excluded." The Yanktons voted down the Wheeler-Howard constitution and remained a subagency of Rosebud until 1963, when they gained full federal recognition (Hoover 64).

The exclusion and frustrations Bonnin felt were part of the price paid for her early education and removal from tribal life. She sacrificed her tribal, communal self for the larger purposes of Indians in American society and to help lay the foundations of Native intellectual traditions (Warrior 10).

Gertrude Bonnin spent the last few years of her life in poverty and despair. Her husband, Raymond, who had legal education but was never formally admitted to the bar, worked to secure representation contracts of Western tribes before Congress and other federal negotiations. The couple's debts mounted. Additionally, their son, Raymond Ohiya, who was diabetic, was in poor health and unable to care for his own children. Their two older grandchildren came to live with them in Virginia. Day after day, the couple plodded to congressional offices and Bureau of Indian Affairs offices, attempting to get a representation contract for Ute claims. In the spring of 1937, Ohiya's poor health forced him, his wife, and other two children to live with the family, as well. While Ohiya unsuccessfully looked for employment, his mother's health began to decline.

Meanwhile, back in Utah, William Hanson revived *The Sun Dance Opera.* His former associate, John Hand, was then director of the New York Opera Guild. The guild chose the opera for performance in the spring of 1938 as opera of the year. Twenty-five years after the original premier, Hanson claimed the opera as his own, noting Bonnin's collaboration only in the program notes.

Interestingly, Gertrude Bonnin does not mention the opera at all in her diaries. Her primary concern was with Raymond, her family, and the legal status of the Ute claims. Her last diary entry is Tuesday, August 17, 1937, five months before her death: "R[aymond] left *early* to town to work . . . on the Ute coal bill. Ohiya went too. He went without kissing goodby."

Gertrude Bonnin died in Washington DC on January 26, 1938. Raymond died in 1942. They are buried in Arlington Cemetery. The legacy she leaves is as vast as the changes she experienced during her lifetime. As an author, she transcribed oral tradition and experience, fiercely guarding her Indian identity and defying the aims of assimilist education. She found an eloquence to articulate historical injustices with an emotional rhetoric that enchanted sympathetic readers and

Stories

audiences. Like Charles Eastman and Luther Standing Bear, but with a female voice, she recorded her transition from a traditional culture through the Indian boarding school to a world of modernity. She utilized the education that alienated her from her roots to empower Native Americans politically.

Gertrude Simmons Bonnin led a complex life at a crucial time for American Indians in this country. Her early writings marked a literary transition from dependence on editors and translators to an autonomous voice—a voice that recounted the injustices of assimilative practices and gained the attention and support of reformers. Her life was full of alienation and disappointment, struggles and vehement writings. Despite the affiliations she maintained with Yanktons and with Utes, her tribal self was finally sacrificed in service to her lifelong efforts. She has no direct living descendants. Some of her actions are rejected by some contemporary tribal peoples. Nevertheless, she remains "yours for the Indian cause."

Stories

Gertrude Bonnin's published stories represent writings from a very short period of her life. In a burst of creativity and popular acclaim, she presented traditional stories from her culture and experiences from her contemporary life as a student and teacher, all the while creating her artistic persona, Zitkala-Ša. Old Indian Legends was published in 1901. Although American Indian Stories was issued in 1921, three-fourths of the volume were reprints of articles that had appeared in periodicals from 1900 to 1902.[1]

When Bonnin returned to the Yankton Reservation at age twenty-four, she seemed committed to a literary career. She wrote to Carlos Montezuma:

> As for my plans—I do not mean to give up my literary work—but while the old people last I want to get from them their treasured ideas of life.
>
> This I can do by living among them. Thus I mean to divide my time between teaching and getting story material. (February 20, 1901)

Despite this commitment and her writing efforts, the realities of life intervened. Financial and familial demands and isolation in Utah may have contributed to Bonnin's public silence. She apparently continued writing, though. Her publications were sparse and did not have the national exposure of her early autobiographical essays and stories. The writings that appeared under the auspices of the Society of American Indians would have had a limited audience. She wrote prolifically while editor of the society's American Indian Magazine (1918–19), but by that time she had turned almost entirely to expository writing.

Most of the stories that appear here are undated. However, they seem to be prepared for publication, as the title pages often indicate word counts. Like her other published stories, the subject matter of these stories is both a recounting of traditional tales and a social commentary. However, the stories here seem less polished and not as tight. Traditional Sioux heroes appear, and, in several of the stories, completely different plot lines seem somewhat unconnected, often with a late appearance of the trickster, Iktomi, or Iya, the giant monster eater. Animal helpers, often in groups of four, interact to aid the heroes/protagonists.

Most of these stories are longer than those that appear in Old Indian Legends. These differences beg the questions of how much editing was required by the original Ginn publishers and if one of the reasons that the current stories were not published in their present form was that they did not meet the literary expectations of contemporary trends. Additionally, the tenor of some of the stories is more violent or sinister than the childlike stories of Old Indian Legends. Although the tone and structure are consistent with Sioux worldview and oral tradition, they may not have been compatible with mainstream standards or with the nonsavage image Bonnin wished to portray to what she assumed would be a non-Indian readership.

Another puzzlement is the source of these stories. Are these a product of Bonnin's intended story-gathering? If so, is their source the various Sioux of Standing Rock, where she temporarily clerked in 1901–02? Or are these stories from her Yankton friends and family? Unfortunately, the answers to these questions will most likely never be known.

Unlike Ella Deloria's Dakota Texts, which are clearly ethnographic in recording and translation, Bonnin's stories seem to be shaped with a literary purpose, again influenced by sentimental rhetoric of her time.[2] As Mary Stout observes: "That [Zitkala-Ša] reinterpreted [a] story in order to transmute the oral narrative aesthetic to the literary one, and to adapt it to an audience containing non-Sioux, is not inconsistent with an oral tradition in which various versions of a tale, imbued with the storyteller's style and suited to the audience of the event, are found" (305). Perhaps this literary purpose is most obvious in "Squirrel Man and His Double," which exists in the original Dakota language in Bonnin's handwriting and in her retelling in "The Witch Woman."

The final stories in this section shift from oral tradition to social commentary. If, as it appears, these were written prior to the last selection, "Dreams," in 1919, it can be argued that Gertrude Bonnin eventually found directness more effective for achieving her aim of justice for Indian peoples.

The Buffalo Woman

Bonnin introduces sacred ceremonies and emblems—central to Sioux worldviews—creating harmony between humans and "four-legged and fur-bearing beings" (Gill and Sullivan 336). This story is similar in structure and content to the familiar Sioux stories of Pte, the White Buffalo Woman, most well known from Black Elk's rendition in Black Elk Speaks *(1–6).[1] Zitkala-Ša's telling of the story does not mention the familiar origin aspect of the bringing of the sacred pipe. She includes structural mythic elements in the story, such as rival brothers in the first section and, later, the forbidden word. The son of the Buffalo Woman and the young man, Wearing Plume, mediates to rescue his father. Escaping the "mischievous" designs of his mother-in-law and proving his virtue, Wearing Plume, again with the assistance of his son, becomes Southern man and leader of his tribe.*

There were once two brother friends who were seldom seen apart. They were not real brothers but had chosen each other after the manner of young men among the Dakotas. Thus they lived going to the hunt and to war together. One had struck an enemy and gained a name. This one always wore the wing feather of a white crane in his braid and so he was called Wearing Plume. The other brother was a fine hunter. He was known as Chaska, or "the elder son." After Wearing Plume had struck a Chippewa and gained his name, Chaska was not seen with him so much as formerly. After one noon they again went hunting together. As they were walking on the prairie they discovered two buffaloes, a bull, and a cow. They stalked these buffaloes, and Wearing Plume's arrow killed the bull. When they were skinning the bull Wearing Plume said, "Hoye, brother, I indeed wish for the loin sinews of this bull. I am making a war bow of the young ash."

"But," said Chaska, "I also wish for that sinew on both sides."

"Then I shall take the shoulder sinew," said Wearing Plume.

"I wish to keep those sinews for my father," replied the brother.

"Then," said Wearing Plume, "I will take the shank sinews."

"But I also wish those for my arrow bindings," urged Chaska.

Wearing Plume wiped his knife upon the grass and put the weapon in its sheath. "Friend," he said, "you shall take all of this buffalo. I will go after the one that escaped."

Immediately Wearing Plume set out upon the trail of the cow buffalo. This trail led to the north. He came within sight of the buffalo at midday but could not get within arrow shot. When he ran to the top of a hill where the buffalo had disappeared, he always saw the buffalo upon the next hill ahead.

He became weary and footsore with travel, and could hardly drag his feet forward. When the sun was near to setting, the buffalo had disappeared. He could not find the tracks.

While he stood upon a hill looking in every direction, suddenly he saw a fine tepee upon the prairie not far away.

Wearing Plume went to this tepee. He found there a very fine woman dwelling alone. The woman bade him enter, and set papa and wasna before him.[2] She had an abundance of food and the hunter ate until satisfied. In the evening the woman removed her moccasins and oiled her feet with bear's oil. In this way a woman shows respect to her husband.

Wearing Plume understood that this beautiful woman was willing to become his wife, when she should arrive among her people. He slept outside her tepee, but in the morning the tepee and the woman were gone. All traces of them had vanished.

Again he saw the buffalo going northward in the distance. He followed as before. All day he followed but could not catch the buffalo. At night the buffalo disappeared and again he saw the tepee of the beautiful woman who served his hunger before.

Wearing Plume understood that a great mystery had happened. During four days he followed the buffalo and slept

8

beside the woman's tepee. Then he persuaded the woman to return with him to his people. She did so and there became his wife. The people knew that Wearing Plume had married a buffalo woman and they rejoiced greatly. Whenever they wanted meat, this woman went out on the prairie and called the buffalo near to their village, so that they had meat and robes in plenty.

All the people paid this buffalo woman great respect. They did all things that she commanded. When this woman bore a son, Wearing Plume's relatives gave a great feast. "For now," they said, "we shall always have the buffalo people among us, and we shall thus become a great nation."

The buffalo woman loved her husband and his relatives, and she ruled the people wisely. She laid only one command upon them, that no one should ever mention the name of Tagu, who was grandfather king of the buffaloes.[3] This aged one was sacred to all his kind, and once a tribe of people should mention his name no more buffaloes would travel in their country. This command the buffalo woman gave to her village to show her love for and confidence in her husband and his people.

Thus a number of winters were passed in peace and plenty. Then one day a great number of buffaloes came off the prairie and ran down the hills near to the village. The hunters made a surround and killed a great number of buffaloes. Only one hairless old bull escaped. This hairless old bull was Tagu, grandfather of the buffaloes.

Some boys, crazed by excitement, chased this venerable one. "Ho! Ho! Ho!" shouted a reckless one. "This may indeed be Tagu. Let us kill the old rascal, at any rate!"

The buffalo woman heard this shout. She assisted Tagu to escape. Then she struck her tepee and gathered all her clothing in a bundle. When the people saw this they were much moved. They gathered about the wife of Wearing Plume and begged her to remain among them. But she would not. She made her things in a large pack and, taking her little son with her, went northward. Though the people offered her their finest paints and all their chief ornaments, they could not detain her. Though they followed after her with presents, she would accept nothing.

When Wearing Plume came in from the hunt to find his wife gone, he took his weapons and immediately followed her. After much travel he saw her a long way ahead. He could not easily overtake her, and when he did, she did not notice his presence and would answer nothing to his words.

So the man followed his wife humbly, walking at a distance behind her. This had never happened to any Dakota before. Soon the husband noticed that all the streams which the buffalo woman crossed instantly became dry.

The man became very thirsty, and knew that he must soon perish. When he was about to fall from exhaustion, his young son stopped secretly behind the mother and spoke to him.

"Father," said the boy, "you must indeed be suffering from thirst, since my mother causes all the streams to go dry. When we cross the next stream, follow my foot prints and you will find water in the heel marks."

Wearing Plume did as the boy said and so found water to quench his thirst. After many days, the buffalo woman, seeing how much her husband loved her, repented, and again talked with her husband.

"Let us now go to my people, seeing that I can no longer live with yours," she said.

After a time they came to a new country. One day as they were walking in this country of hills, the buffalo woman said to her husband: "Lo, yonder is my grandfather coming. Make yourself to hide in this tall grass and I will go on to meet him."

When they had approached each other the grandfather said, "How, my granddaughter it appears that I smell something strange."

The woman laughed. "Perhaps a flower," she said.

"We hear that you are married and have lived among the Dakotas," said the old man. "Doubtless you have fetched much blue paint and tobacco." Blue is the favorite paint among buffalo people. The woman opened her pack and gave some to the old man. When she arrived among her people, the woman gave them much blue paint and tobacco. They were greatly pleased, and when she told about her husband and child who had followed her, they bade her fetch them to the village where they should be well treated.

So this was done, and Wearing Plume came to live with the buffalo people. All the people were well contented, except his mother-in-law. This wicked old woman hated her daughter's husband, and continually sought means to destroy him. She went about saying mischievous things, and talking evilly among her friends, and thus she poisoned the minds of many against her son-in-law.

One day, speaking of a certain medicine woman, she said to her daughter, "This Mysterious Owl is an evil talker.[4] She was telling me last night that the people were going to have a dance and she said, 'If your son-in-law can not dance a whole day, they will trample him in the earth.'"

In the morning it came about as she had said. The drum sounded first the slow rat-tat-tat-tat-tat of the waking time and then, Boom-bom! Boom-bom!, the swift beat of the dance music.

Immediately these strange buffalo people began to act very crazily. They ran hither and thither knocking each other and their tepees to the earth. They came into the dance circle thus leaping and shouting. They sang a crazy song thus: "La-la-la-la-la-la, tatanka ohitika miye wahiye!" (Here am I the brave buffalo!) The buffalo woman's husband, who was called The Southern Man, knew that he must dance this dance with a strong endurance and a fearless heart or perish. He had two medicines. One of them was anise-root which he put in his mouth to keep down his thirst. The other was a green powder with which he painted his body.

He also wore an arrow, sharply pointed at both ends, across his breast and attached to sinews hung about his neck. This was to defend himself against rude jostling. Before he began dancing he looked at the sky and prayed to Wakinyan, spirit of thunders. Then he called his son to him privately and gave him some instructions. "Come very near to the dancers about midday and shout my name. Say to the people, 'My father is somebody in the South country; when he becomes dusty with dancing the thunder people will cause a rain to fall for the washing and refreshing of his body.'"

The man began dancing. He shook a medicine rattle and danced with violent exertion. After a time the dust and heat were suffocating. The buffalo people whirled about him, leaping, one above the other. The buffalo chant rose above the heavy roll of the drum. A man fell and was instantly trampled to death under the heel—for this was the law of the dance.

"One!" shouted The Southern Man, so that every one heard his voice. "Two!" Another went down and was beaten into the earth. The Southern Man was dancing violently as at first. His breath was coming in gasps; his body was buried in dust, and he was looking upward to the sky.

Then a clear voice, the voice of his son, rang high above all the noises of the dance, shouting the words of the father's bidding. When the boy had ceased crying, a deep mutter of thunder shook the earth, and rain fell until the people danced in water. Thus The Southern Man was made new and continued the dance without harm.

When the sun was about to set a man fell and died. "Three!" shouted The Southern Man. He ran between two strong chiefs and, stooping, cut them across the middle. "Four-Five!" he shouted.

The buffalo people saw that this man was wakan. They ceased dancing. The buffalo woman loved her husband more than ever. She caused him to be made war chief of the tribe.

When the Buffalo Herd Went West

This story is only one account of the origin of the buffalo on the plains. As a fundamental source of both food and stories for Plains Indians, the buffalo was crucial; the decimation of these animals was catastrophic. An unnamed Indian woman appears to be the hero figure of the story, but once her ailing husband recovers, they work together, expressing the gender complementarity of Plains Indians.[1] The moral of the tale rewards generosity and punishes greed. The man's power comes from the sacred emblems of Buffalo medicine: the drum, flute, deer-hoof rattles, and the sounds they make. The screech of the owl only adds to the man's power (Walker, Lakota Belief and Ritual, *46).*

Like Ella Deloria's story "The Buffalo People," this tale has a sense of timelessness because of its setting in the mythological past and continuing influences on Sioux worldview (see Rice, Ella Deloria's The Buffalo People, *94–126).*

Zitkala-Ša concludes her rendering of the tale by introducing Iktomi, the Sioux trickster, and reiterating the central theme. The trickster is a complicated figure who, through humor, misbehavior, and negative example, socializes moral behavior.[2]

From a teepee among the trees, an Indian woman came forth to gather the seed-fruit of the wild rose. It was early springtime. Great white clouds drifted in the sky. Her hunter husband, crippled by accident in a buffalo chase, lay within the teepee, slowly recovering. Every day his faithful wife gathered the rose berries and cooked them. It was all the food they had.

While picking the red berries from the thorny bush one day, she heard a distant noise of hurrying hoof beats upon the ground. Looking up quickly in the direction from which the sound came, she beheld a man mounted on a snow white pony, chasing a maddened buffalo. Her bewildered eyes, as they lit upon the roaring shaggy buffalo, seemed to draw his course straight toward her. On came the buffalo and the man on the white pony in hot pursuit. Instinctively she jumped behind a near tree for protection. Close at her feet the buffalo fell dead!

The man, dismounting, said in undisguised surprise, "Oh how came you here?" The Indian woman stood silent by the tree, her protector. She was loathe to speak to a stranger. The hunter did not wait for her reply. "You shall have choice meat, if you wait here and watch me cut up the buffalo," he said as he flourished a knife.

She watched him disrobe the dead buffalo and cut his bones asunder. He talked loud and fast all the while. He boasted of his prowess as a hunter and his unsurpassed skill with the knife. He claimed that he could carve a buffalo in the twinkling of an eye. He told of his wonderful generosity, how he always gave the choicest meats to the sick and hungry. Never a moment did he lose in his self praise. Having finished the carving of the buffalo he carried the meat, piece by piece, and packed it on his pony. The Indian woman who had waited, looking wistfully upon the tender steak, had said in her heart, "I will broil it upon the red hot coals for my sick husband." Now there was nothing left for her. The man of empty words, ready to go, tossed the tripe away, as if throwing it to a dog. He said, "Take that and make a good soup." Leading his pony laden with much meat, he went his way.

The woman hurried to her husband in the teepee and told him all that had happened. Carefully she washed the tripe and dashing boiling water upon it removed the outer skin until it was every whit clean and white. Over the center fire she cooked it quickly. It made a savory soup. Famished for long weary days, they ate the soup with a relish. The husband said he felt himself growing stronger. Both rejoiced that before long he would be able to go again in the hunt. Then they would have all the buffalo meat and venison that they could eat and some to share with their neighbors, somewhere in the big world.

It was after this occurrence, the soup having been eaten up, they were again very hungry. The woman went out to gather the rose berries. Her trained eye spied the same strange hunter, on his fleet white pony, chasing another buffalo! Again he killed it and began at once to cut it up. She was hungry but coveted the buffalo meat more for her sick husband than for herself. She stood close by, watching the strange man and his plunder. He chattered and chattered like a magpie. "I am the greatest hunter in the world. I am the most generous man in the world. I always give away the choicest pieces. I have great food bags stored in my teepee. I never hunger." Again, as he talked, he packed all the meat away, only the tripe, which he tossed aside, saying, "Take that and make soup with it."

This time, the woman became indignant and said, "Whoever you may be, you are the most unkind man in the world. You are a man of empty words. You boast of giving choice meat to the sick and poor, but instead you keep the best portion, only giving away the tripe. Now I am going to tell this to my husband, who is a medicine man. He will get his sacred drum, sing his mystery song, and no buffalo will come nigh you. He will scare the buffalo away from you."

The stranger shook with a sudden palsy—"Yun! Yun! Yun!" He groaned in pain. "Do not tell him! Do not let him bring his drum. I fear only four things in this world. These are the drum, flute, deer hoof rattles, and the screech owl. Do not let him bring any of these four wakan things and I will give you much meat. Every day I will come chasing the buffalo." He gave the woman all the meat she could carry. She went home and told her husband what had happened. He listened attentively. Being a man who understood many mysteries of the invisible power, he at once knew the stranger was misusing some sacred gift. "Let him fulfill his promises," he said.

But the man with the white pony failed to return. The Dakota and his wife again were without food. They made a drum and a deer hoof rattle. They traveled across a prairie in search of that man of empty words. With these four fears they would destroy him. They found his teepee. They approached it straight as an arrow flies and took their places on either side of the entrance way. The woman shook the deer hoof rattle and blew upon the flute; the man beat upon the sacred drum and hooted like an owl.

Out rushed the man of empty words, with his fingers stopping his ears. Like a mad man, he ran, shrieking, into the thick woods. The man and wife cautiously lifted the teepee door and peered into the cone shaped dwelling. The walls were lined with great food bags—bags that were decorated handsomely with beads and porcupine quills. They were filled to brim with dried meats and dried fruits and roots.

They entered in. From a tall pole hung a large bladder beautifully embroidered in the most wonderful designs with brightly colored quills. Ordinarily plain and undecorated bladders were filled with beef tallow and put away in the food bags. Very queer indeed that one should be decorated and hung upon a pole at the center of the teepee. This was certainly unusual. The man scrutinized it from a safe distance, reading some of the old symbols worked upon it. At last he whispered to his wife. "This appears to me like a powerful magic bag. It may be one of the ancient bags made at the beginning of the world." Nodding her head in assent, the wife gazed on the large bladder. It was very old; its skin was tough and wrinkled. It was tied at the neck with the sinews of the moose.

Many moons they lived in this teepee, where there was an abundance of dried meats and fruits. The man was now fully recovered, but one thing troubled them. It was the magic bag hanging overhead! Sometimes this bladder became agitated. It swayed to and fro upon the string when there was no wind blowing without the teepee. At such times a tumultuous murmur as of many voices and noises issued from the bladder. There were sounds of hoof beats and the rumble of trampling herds, the bellowing of the buffalo mingled with the neighing of horses; far away shouts of men and women above the rattle of drum and clatter of gourds, dogs barking and coyotes howling. There seemed to be a faint trembling of the earth.

At such times the man and his wife sat in profound awe, eyeing the swaying old bladder. They burnt sweet herbs in smoke prayers to the Great Spirit.

At length their food bags were empty. They began to talk of going on a long hunt. One day as the sun hung low in the west, the woman went into the nearby woods to bring some sticks for the camp fire. She went about picking up fagots here and there. She came upon an old decayed log lying across her way. There, hiding under this log lay a frightened old man, the man of empty words.

He was terribly afraid at sight of her. He screeched out, "He! He! He! Do not harm me! Listen! In my teepee you have seen a bladder hanging. When you are out of meat you must untie the neck of the bladder and open it a little way. A buffalo will come out. Open it a little farther and a white pony will come out. Then close the bladder and let your husband mount the white pony and chase the buffalo. Thus you will always have plenty of meat."

Astounded by the man hiding like a culprit in the wildwood and who, begging for his life, told the sacred secret about the bladder, which no man dared to betray—she looked quickly around on all sides, like a deer, alert to see if any object moved in the quiet landscape. She turned to look again at the man. She saw nothing but an artichoke weed. She returned to the teepee and told her husband all she had seen and heard in the woods.

"Well then, let us open the magic bladder!" said he. They took it carefully down from the pole, carried it out of doors, and unloosed the neck of the bladder. Immediately a wild buffalo ran out, bellowing and pawing upon the earth, and a white pony followed closely behind.

They tied the bladder and the man caught the white pony, mounted it without saddle or bridle, and chased and killed the buffalo! Thus they had meat and skins in plenty. Never in their whole lives had they tasted such savory, tender meat. They talked together of sharing their game with their people. The man praised the fleetness of the pony's feet. He had never before mounted such a steed! He traveled like the wind! "At day break tomorrow I will ride him again. I shall go forth to invite the world to feast with us. For tonight I have tied the pony to our teepee pole that no prowling enemy may steal him away."

The next day the first streak of dawn awoke them. Their first thought was of the white pony. They went out together to water him at the river. He was gone! Only the rawhide rope remained tied to the tent at one end and a loop large enough for a horse's neck at the other. There was no track or sign of him save a white fleck in the sky. "I guess he is that white cloud in the sky! He is gone beyond our reach," sighed the man in deep regret.

Still, as the sun rose higher and higher, the man thought more and more about the white pony, saying, "I shall go on foot to invite the world and perhaps I may come upon the white pony on my way." He left his teepee.

During his absence, a tall, gaunt, man-like creature appeared at the oval teepee door. The Indian woman recognized old Iktomi, the mischief maker of camps.[3] Unguardedly she told him of the white pony. She asked him if he had seen it on his way hither. "No, I have not seen any horse at all," Iktomi answered, twisting and twisting his neck, looking upward at the mystery pouch. He grew wild with curiosity. He startled her by suddenly declaring "I am going to open the mystery pouch! I want a buffalo to hunt and a white pony to ride." Oh hateful Iktomi, Mischief Maker! He always spoiled the happiness of others. In spite of her pleas not to touch the sacred bag, he strode roughly by her; he pushed her aside, saying, "You told me about its magic, now I am going to try it." He took down the magic pouch and carried it out of doors. In his haste to untie the neck of the bladder, his clumsy fingers dropped the pouch to the ground! It fell wide open. Instantly a great herd of buffalo stampeded! A herd so great that it was impossible to number them. They rushed by, in a mad fury, bellowing shrilly and roaring with a voice of thunder. Under their hoofs the earth shook. They trampled upon Iktomi, the woman, and the tent. This, they say, is when the buffalo herd went west.

Buzzard Skin and the Sea Monsters

*Zitkala-Ša tells another story in which Iktomi appears at the reso-
lution as a* deus ex machina. *Here the trickster exposes the
duplicity of the hero, Hepasu, or Buzzard Skin. Hepasu must rescue Badger from the evil forces of* Unktehi, *the Water Monsters.[1]
The malevolent Water Monsters cannot recognize Hepasu in his
buzzard disguise, and Hepasu bravely enters the dangerous world.
However, Hepasu and Badger pay for their own trickery finally by
being confined to their natural homes. The story explains the close
range of the badger, and by implication contrasts the badger with
the free-roaming buffalo. In defining the virtues and limitations
of the badger, this tale is a type of origin story.*

Hepasu lived with his friend, the badger. Hepasu was a hunter.
He had an art by which he always knew where to find game
and how to foil his enemies. Hepasu daily brought deer meat
and deer skins to their dwelling. The badger stayed at home to
tan the skins and to gather sticks for the evening fires, on
whose dried embers he broiled the tasty venison.

One evening Hepasu came in from hunting to find an
empty teepee. The badger was gone. The ashes were cold and
dead in the fire place. No where was there a trace of the badger.
Hepasu searched for his lost friend two whole days. There was
a great marsh near their dwelling. Hepasu believed that his
friend, who was low of stature, must have gotten lost in the tall
grass of the marsh. Thither Hepasu went, looking for the badger within the deep grass of the marsh.

As Hepasu was wading waist deep in the tall grass, he
heard the sound of girls' voices in a song. Stealthily he crept
toward them until he spied two beautiful girls sitting near the
water's edge. Hepasu held his breath and listened. He over-

heard them talking of someone whom the warriors of their tribe had captured.

One of the girls sang with a flutelike voice a bravery song. "Bravely our warriors seized him. Bravely they brought him, captive to our camp. Badger is his name—name of the captive."

Hepasu rushed in upon the innocent girls, and caught each by the nape of the neck. They cried out with fright. These young girls were of the tribe of Water Rails, the Shiyantankana. Holding them fast, Hepasu asked, "Who took the badger captive? Tell me his name."

The older sister answered, "The badger was hunting and sat on the sand bar to rest. He was captured by our warriors."

"We heard the Sea Monsters have taken him into their earth lodge under the bottom of the lake," ventured the younger, looking at Hepasu with wild round eyes.

Hepasu released the girls. He returned to his dwelling. He made two long arrows with sharp teeth—he dipped them into deadly poison. The next morning he went to the sand bar, where he heard that the Sea Monster, Unktehi, came to play and to sleep upon the sand at midday. Here he dug a pit, and hid himself in it. At noon he heard the noise of boiling and tumbling waters. He heard a gruff voice say, "Shee.² Husband, see this heap of sand! It was not here yesterday."

"Hoh!" grumbled a still coarser voice. "Do you fear a heap of sand?" Then the talking ceased. It became quiet. Soon Hepasu heard the deep water monsters snoring heavily. He jumped out of his hiding place and shot his long arrows. Each of the monsters was pierced behind the ear. Hepasu dived out of sight again into his pit. He heard the wounded ones groaning with pain and floundering about in the water, descending into their den under the lake.

When the monsters had disappeared, Hepasu saw the water red with their blood. "They may die," he thought as he returned to his tent that evening. Next day he was walking on the sands of the lake shore when a buzzard appeared in the near distance. This buzzard was a medicine man. He carried a great bag of herbs and roots. He had a sacred red gourd tied upon his head. He was stalking straight toward the lake. With every step he pronounced magic words, "Kha-khe, Khi-Khi!" with a croaking voice. He had come a long way and was tired. He sat down on the sand to rest.

Hepasu boldly approached him, "Grandfather, where are you going?" he asked.

"I have been summoned to the deep water monsters' lodge. Unktehi and his wife were wounded yesterday by a hidden enemy. I have a powerful medicine which heals all wounds. I am going there to cure them," replied the medicine man, the buzzard.

The buzzard started away. No sooner was his back turned than Hepasu threw a rock and killed him. Hepasu skinned the buzzard and clothed himself in its skin and feathers. He wore the head with the red gourd tied to it like a hood. He looked like the old medicine man, the buzzard. Like him he began the chant as he directed his steps toward the deep water monsters' cave. "Khe-khe! Khi-khi!"

"Heca, the buzzard is coming!" cried the water people to each other. They rejoiced to see this renowned medicine man arrive. They opened the door of the earth lodge and stood aside to let the medicine man enter. Lo, the Buzzard Skin entered into the sick room.

As Hepasu passed within, he saw his lost friend, the badger, tied securely with rawhide ropes to a strong post driven deep into the ground. The badger, lying near the doorway, was very pale from hunger and the fear of death. From the corner of an eye, Buzzard Skin saw the deep water folk kick the lean ribs of the badger as they passed by the door. They treated him like a cur. They abused him shamefully.

"Hehe, misun!" muttered the medicine man. "My poor little brother." No one understood what he said. They thought they were magic words to heal the wounded monsters.

Hepasu looked about with narrowed eyes as he took his seat in the place of honor. Around the outer circle of the lodge he saw a row of conjurers and medicine men of the Water Clans, who had gathered to witness a great cure performed. These all smoked a long stemmed pipe, which they passed one to another, around the circle. They greeted the medicine man most cordially.

Near the center of this big earth lodge under the lake, the monsters lay upon their seaweed mats, shamelessly groaning aloud. Hepasu's arrows were sticking in their necks.

Hepasu, smugly cloaked in the buzzard hood and robe, now examined their wounds, stooping and blowing his breath upon them. He chanted a magic song. Chewing healing herbs, he blew upon them. Still the monsters, large as the biggest buffalo and with long wide ears like some gigantic rabbit, writhed and groaned with pain unbearable. The medicine had no effect. The onlookers became very still.

Then Hepasu addressed them with a most solemn face and mien. "Good people, my medicine never fails! However I can do nothing so long as any one is within sight or hearing. If you wish your kinsmen to be healed of their wounds, you must all go away to the far side of this lake bottom."

When they were gone, Hepasu rose up out of the deep water and built a fire near the shore. He cut long rods and put the points upon the flames. The fire tipped them with red hot embers. Carrying these burning rods he dove down to the lake bed and entered the monsters' earth lodge. Once more he stooped over the helpless monsters. This time he was in earnest. "Why did you tie my friend, the badger, like a dog to your door post?" He hissed into their ears. He tore the arrows from their necks and thrust the fire brands into the wounds. The monsters fainted away and never more regained consciousness. They were dead.

In his excitement, Hepasu had singed his own Buzzard Skin and feathers. There were great holes burned into it. Releasing the badger, he gave him a bite of dried meat and berries from the small lunch bag on his belt. The badger felt refreshed after eating food. "Now, my friend, we must escape from this under lake region," said Hepasu. In the meanwhile, the water people, anxiously waiting at the far end of the lake, were growing impatient. Iktomi, the spider, had come among them whispering that Hepasu, the badger's friend, had come disguised in the buzzard's feather, and had connived to do them mischief. The water people, listening to Iktomi, became alarmed. They sent the pollywog as a spy to the lodge of the sick monsters to see what the medicine man was doing.

The pollywog discovered Hepasu in disguise as Iktomi had told. He cried aloud "Wan! He—" Hepasu quickly threw a lump of tallow from his lunch bag into the wide open mouth of the pollywog. The fat lodged in his throat. He was nearly choked. With difficulty he swallowed it. Once more the pollywog opened his mouth to call for help, and again, with unerring aim, Hepasu threw another chunk of hard tallow into his throat. The pollywog swallowed fat until he was almost bursting.

A lizard came noiselessly slipping in to spy upon Hepasu. He too opened his mouth to call for help. Hepasu threw lumps of tallow into his mouth until he was choked.

"My friend, you are strong now, let us make our escape before another spy is sent. Let us go home quickly before the water people come back," Hepasu said to the badger. Together they ran from the earth lodge under the lake and came into the crystal waters over head. Before they had gone far, they were surrounded. Snakes, frogs, fish, and water bugs attacked them. Hepasu and the badger fought for their lives. They prevailed over these people, thrusting them aside and killing great numbers. Narrowly escaping, they reached their tent in safety. Since then the badger does not wander very far from his teepee.

The Hawk Woman

The hero of "The Hawk Woman" is Cetan, *also known as the hawk spirit, whose reputation was for swiftness and endurance (Walker,* Lakota Belief, *122). He performs the hero's quest: leaving home with animal helpers, going on a journey, acquiring a wife and posterity, and, finally, restoring order to his home community. The tools Cetan obtains to conquer his sister, the evil Hawk Woman, are not his but gifts to his twin sons. Like his offspring, the story is symmetrical in its presentation. He defeats Hawk Woman not only through his heroic efforts of strength and trickery but with the communal contributions of animal helpers and family. The animals, a field mouse, a cougar, a brown hawk, a rattlesnake, and an owl, reflect wildlife indigenous to the Plains.*

Cetan, a handsome young brave, offended by the ways of his eccentric sister, bade his father and mother farewell. He wished to go forth into the big world of wonders and seek his own fate. Sitting in a round boat of rawhide, he drifted downstream.

At nightfall, he landed in a strange place. He was unafraid, for everywhere under the sky was home to him. He made camp. That very night he had many callers. He was visited by a field mouse, a cougar, a brown hawk, a rattle snake, and an owl. All these wished to be called his children, and to go with him on his journey until each should find a country better suited to his liking.

Cetan consented.

On the following day, they all got into his boat and paddled down the river. They came upon a country where there were many hickory trees, wild carrots, and "beans" growing. "This suits me!" exclaimed the field mouse.

"Here then you shall live," said Cetan, and he put the field mouse ashore.

In parting, the mouse said, "Father, when you return this way, I shall have a present ready for you."

The next day, they came upon a country of high hills and rock ledges. "I like this," exclaimed the rattle snake, sounding his rattles. Here he was landed. He also promised a fine present.

In the country of swamps and lakes, where water fowl were plentiful, the brown hawk flew away. When they were passing through a heavily wooded region where there was much vegetation and mice, and small animals were numerous, the owl departed. In an open country where the streams were skirted with timber and deer were frequently seen, the cougar stopped to camp. Each promised a present upon Cetan's return.

Cetan had not really thought about returning. He was mystified that all these wild people continually talked of his return, when they would bestow their offerings of love and gratitude.

As last Cetan reached a village where the people were very poor. At sight of them, his heart grew tender with pity. He landed. Stepping up to an old woman's teepee, he asked why the people were so miserable and starving.

The old stooped grandmother began wailing, "My grandchild, my grandchild, we have met with a sad fate. Our enemies have frightened away all the buffalo. There is no game to hunt. We are starving to death."

Cetan asked for an old buffalo robe he saw within her teepee. It seemed like taking her last possession from her. He was a stranger, too. Yet the old woman did not hesitate to give it gladly. Thanking her, Cetan took the buffalo robe out on the open prairie and scraped the thick black hair off, scattering it to the four winds. Then he built a smudge of sweet grass. He stood with his hands toward the sun and called aloud to the buffalo herds to return hither. On that same evening great herds of buffalo came grazing upon the prairie grass. With a shout of joy, the men rushed out and came back with choicest meat and buffalo robes.

There was singing and dancing in the camp. The people became strong and prosperous. Cetan was honored with a special feast. The chieftain, admiring the young man who had so wonderfully saved his camp through his compassion for them, sent his warriors to ask him to live with them forever. He suggested that he would make him his son-in-law by giving him his favorite daughter to wed. Cetan was pleased with the words of the chieftain, for he had seen this beautiful young daughter and loved her much. He remembered how shyly she had smiled, when as onlookers at a dance, their eyes met by chance.

Cetan lived in this village two winters. He lived happily with his beautiful wife. Twin boys were born to them. When these babies got old enough to sit up alone and to creep around, Cetan said to his wife, "My heart beats hard at times, and I fear my old parents are sick or in dire distress. I feel that I must go to their aid."

The young wife, hugging her black haired twin babies, replied, "These little men say, 'Ate, Father, we are going with you. We want to be kind to our grandmother and grandfather, especially if they are crying for help.'"

They took their children and went in their rawhide boat up the great river.

When they reached the country of the cougar, Cetan beheld him sitting upon the bank. "Come to land, Father," the cougar hailed him. "I have brought presents for my little twin brothers!" They came ashore and the cougar gave two little fawn skins, very beautiful and soft. "These are your covering my wee brothers," he said and spread them lightly upon the babies.

When they reached the thick wooded country where the wild carrots grew, the owl flew to meet them, bringing blankets of tiny mole skins. "I have brought these blankets for my baby brothers, whom I love," he said.

Next came the brown hawk from the land of lakes and swamps. He also brought little robes made of the green feathers of mallards' heads. He too loved his little baby brothers.

In the country of rocks, the rattle snake showed himself, beckoning the boat ashore. He had pouches of fluffy red down plucked from the breasts of birds. "These feathers are for pillows upon which my twin brothers may rest in sleep," he said.

Still farther on, they stopped to visit the field mouse. He brought a large bag filled with wild rice and dried roots. "This will make a fine broth for my little brothers," he said. He stroked the babies' dimpled fingers, as dearly did he love them.

Now at last, Cetan arrived with his family at the place of his former home. The people were gone, and the camp ground deserted. His heart beat hard. Some enemy had destroyed them utterly perchance. At the outskirts of the old camp ground he saw a small smoke stained teepee near a clump of plum trees in blossom. He and his wife, each carrying a baby boy, approached this solitary teepee. "It is so lonely, I fear it is a burying place for the dead," whispered the twin boys' mother.

"We shall soon see," gravely answered Cetan. He now understood his father and mother had been overtaken by some terrible evil. The white blossoms of the plum trees alone held out hope by their presence in the midst of the ruins.

Cautiously, Cetan lifted the door flap and peered in. He saw two old people sitting with bowed heads, crouching and fearful of every motion and sound. When Cetan spoke, they winced like ones accustomed to being beaten. "Ina, Ate, Mother, Father," he began. "With my wife and our twin babies, I have returned." Reaching forth his right hand, he waited for their response—to shake hands in greeting. Timidly, the old toothless woman placed her thin fevered hand into his strong cool palm. Then she wept for joy. The old father too put out his withered hand and tried to grasp firmly the hand of his long absent son, now returned.

"What has brought death to the village? What has driven you into this lonely dwelling?" Cetan asked. "What has made the scars upon your faces? Why have you cut your hair in mourning?"

The aged parents now told him the terrible story of a wicked, wicked hawk woman, who daily visited them and-burned their faces with firebrands from their center fire. "My son, your sister was bewitched by some unknown power. Soon after you left us, she was changed into a hawk. She flew into the sky screaming like a mad thing, every day coming back to torture us. She has killed the village people, one by one, and now we are the only ones remaining. We beg her in mercy to put an end to our misery but she laughs harshly and continues her daily visitations. Ah! We fear her. She is cruel. She has been asking when you would return! Oh she knows everything. We are afraid that she will harm you and the sweet twin babies and their mother. Every day at noon, this hawk woman comes here. Hide yourself and your family, or else she will surely kill you as she has destroyed our village people."

"That wretched girl! I always felt she was not a real being, that was why I left two years ago. Now, I shall punish her," he said sternly.

Cetan at once prepared a green powdered medicine and with it he painted their bodies. "Do not ask me why I do this," he remarked. "I have my own magic with which I can destroy evil spirits." The sun hung low in the west. The day was nearly done. So weary and sorrow worn were the old father and mother that after they had been anointed with the green medicine, they relaxed into a peaceful slumber. The wife with her baby boys too fell asleep, from fatigue. Cetan also slept.

With the first rays of daylight in the east, the children and their grandparents awoke. All were refreshed from the night's rest. They were happy. The twin boys' mother, not finding any food in the old people's teepee, took some rice and dried roots from the bag presented to the babies on their way. On the center fire she made an appetizing rice broth. All partook of it and were wholly satisfied. "That is the most nourishing rice I have ever eaten," both the old grandmother and grandfather commented.

"It was a present given to our boys by the field mouse," modestly explained the young mother.

"Oh! The dear thing," exclaimed the old grandmother.

As the sun rose higher in the zenith, the old man and woman began to be afraid. "The hawk woman comes here at noon," they repeated. Cetan took the many curious presents that had been given to the twin boys and selected from them certain ones. No one dared question him. He had requested them not to do so.

The little fawn skins he spread over the baby boys on the ground, out of doors. The pouch of red feathers he placed upon the shoulder of his young wife. Taking his stone ax, he stepped out of the teepee and transformed himself into an old stump near the door.

At noon, the hawk woman, shrieking horribly, came down from the sky. As she alighted upon the ground, she looked upon the stump. "This was not here before," she said. Again she looked upon two little fawns playing near the old stump, and she said, "These fawns were never here before." She looked around and seeing a red bird perched upon the plum trees in blossom, the hawk woman said, "This red bird was never here before." She would not go near. She seemed to know the presence of magic. Roughly tossing the oval door flap aside, she stooped forward to enter the teepee. She disappeared within and began as usual to speak cruelly to the old man and the old woman. "Where is Cetan?" she asked them. Before she had time to snatch a firebrand from the center fire to burn the faces of the old folks, Cetan sprang out of his hiding and struck her with his stone ax. As fast as he struck, the stone ax passed through her, as if she were only air, and she remained untouched, unhurt.

Making the sound of a maddened wild beast growling, Cetan reached out his hand at arm's length and began to whirl the stone ax in a circle. His weapon became a circle of magic light, wherein the wicked hawk woman's face grew dim, fading away into nothingness. The circle burst into a red flame and the hawk woman was consumed. Where she had stood were left a few burnt cinders. Her spirit passed like a breath, upward.

Every day at noon this bit of white cloud may be seen floating high overhead.

Cetan folded away the little blankets of fawn skins and the pouch of red feathers. He brought his wife and the twin babies into the teepee where the grandparents were offering up a prayer smoke of sweet herbs for their deliverance.

The black cinders, Cetan gathered and crushed into a powder. He went over the deserted camp, sprinkling the ground with it. Where it fell, life was restored. Tents appeared. Men and women sat around their open fires, sociably eating, chatting, and smoking together. Little mischievous boys and girls played amid shouts of laughter. Ponies grazed quietly near the teepees.

Returning to his old parents, Cetan tenderly brushed their tangled locks, and smoothed them into little slender braids. He dressed them in handsome buckskins and led them to their former dwelling, renewed and ready for their occupation. His old father remembered, like one awakening from a dream, that he was the chief of this camp before the advent of this wicked hawk woman. He was glad, oh, so glad, to be restored to his proper place and rank. He never tired of watching his village people, once more contented and happy.

The Boy and
the Rainbow

The characters in this story are a combination of humanized animals and human beings. Like the other stories, this story has a clear moral about the need to respect what is sacred and the consequences of inappropriate behavior. The son must adhere strictly to ritual prescription. The recitation of the prayer four times is consistent with the sacred nature of the number four. The white owl is the agent of temptation yet exemplifies the power of obedience to ritual. Unlike the Christian worldview, wherein the price of sin is condemnation in an afterlife, the young boy's violation of instructions transforms into something beautiful in the first rainbow, and he assumes his natural form as the loon.

Zitkala-Ša notes that this is a "Devil's Lake Sioux Story." She also records: "Huntka is loon. Wica Tonkana is gull. White Owl's Trail to the north." The rhetoric of the first paragraph clearly shows that she is explaining "medicine men" to an audience who would be unfamiliar with medicine men and their power.

Indian men observing nature discover wonderful secrets in flower, bird, earth, and sky. Those who are most learned are known as great medicine men. Their medicine is their thoughts, their words, and their songs, as well as their herbs and roots.

Huntka's father is one of the greatest of medicine men. His love for his little son often caused him trouble with his magic art. Now again, he found his darling crying as if he were an orphan child and unbeloved. Tears coursed down either bronzed cheek in little wet trails. The great medicine man, fearful lest some evil thing had happened in his absence, anxiously asked, "What has happened? Why do you cry, my son?"

The boy, Huntka, complained through his tears, "I am crying, father, for your medicine. I want to try your magic. I want to call the buffalo herds to me."

"Huntka, my son, you have asked the one thing impossible! The Great Spirit forbids. What I have learned through my own works, I can neither lend nor give to another." Hereupon Huntka began to cry more bitterly. Three days he wept. Three nights he moaned in his sleep, "I want to call the buffalo here to me with your magic."

The father, distressed with the crying of his son, rose from his meditation and went outdoors to the high pole where he kept his medicine bag tied, high above the reach of meddlesome hands. With the greatest care, he selected his herbs and combining them together made his buffalo charm for which his naughty boy was crying. Placing it in the medicine bag, he gave it to the son.

"Remember, my son, to do exactly as I have told you; or else there will follow a terrible punishment for any least part forgot. Select the ground on the hilltop to stand upon during the ceremony. Make the offering of sweet grass smoke. When the smoke prayer ascends straight upward, lift the medicine bag to the sun, directly in front of your face. Repeat this four times. Be very careful of your count. It is important. Then call aloud 'Pte uwa po! Buffalo, come hither!' With this call the ceremony is ended. Hurry home, as fast as your feet can run." With an eager face, beaming with joy, Huntka listened to the words of his father. His eyes were upon the magic bag, save for a momentary glance at his medicine man father.

The words of instruction did not weigh heavily upon the boy. Buoyantly, he hied himself toward the nearest hill, hugging closely the medicine bag. So tightly did he hold it that the beaded designs were imprinted on his chubby arm. Singing and skipping, he let out sudden little hoots of irrepressible glee. He reached the hilltop. Panting, he paused to scan the open country around, in imitation of his father. He began the sacred ceremony.

It was not difficult to remember the words of his father, he thought as he quickly whirled the sticks and made a fire on the ground. He piled sweet grass upon the blaze. Holding the medicine bag toward the sun, he called at the top of his voice "Pte uwa po! Buffalo, come hither!" Playing with his father's magic, he acted like one in a dream. The ceremony was finished. He turned to go home, but his alert eye spied a white owl sitting upon a hill nearby. "Why, there is my dear old grandfather!" he exclaimed in surprise. In those days, Indian boys and girls remembered their kinship to all trees, birds, animals, earth, and sky. It was the most natural thing for Huntka to recognize his grandfather, the white owl of the North country. At sight of him, Huntka forgot all else. He dropped the medicine bag to the ground and ran over to the snow white owl.

"Grandfather, I am so happy today. Sing for me, that I may dance. Sing, sing, grandfather," Huntka coaxed. The great white owl slowly stretched each wing and dropped it again into repose. He tilted his head to get a side squint at the boy, whose blue black hair, braided into ropes, fell forward over his robust chest.

Then the grandfather owl talked to him. "I will sing, my grandchild, to please you. But do not ask me to break the ancient custom, which is to sing only four songs." With this, the white owl picked up a stick and began beating upon the ground, in time with his singing. "Yehehe-yehehehe." The owl repeated these words three times. His voice was very, very deep and had such startling little breaks in it.

Huntka danced furiously; he was wildly excited. "Again, grandfather, sing again!" he shouted at the close of the first song. The owl sang a second, third, and fourth time. Huntka danced like one possessed but was not yet satisfied. "Again, again, grandfather," he called in a high voice. "Sing again!" The white owl ceased his deep, muffled song. He sat silent, blinking upon the dancing boy.

Huntka seized him by the wings and rudely pulled him about. He ruffled the pretty white feathers and annoyed the old grandfather owl. Still Huntka hung upon his wings, ruffling them more and more. "Hoye, grandfather," Huntka insisted, "hoye, sing for me. I want to dance. Forget the count, grandfather. Forget the four."

Again the boy over persuaded his grandfather, as he had his father. He knew they loved him dearly, and he played upon their feelings. So generous were they toward him that they did not demand kind acts of him in return. The boy was young and did not remember his obligations to those he loves. This he had not yet clearly comprehended. He seemed to be all play, laughter, and dance!

The white owl said, "Let go my wings. Stop ruffling them and I will sing." He began to drum upon the ground and to sing. The boy danced harder than ever. His springing feet seemed not to touch the earth. Bounding here and there, he bent forward, swaying first to one side then to the other, head held up proudly and eyes looking keenly everywhere. Now and then, he hooted, with a dimpled hand to his lips to muffle his slender voice.

Suddenly, without warning, a whirlwind descended upon him. A dark cloud dropped from the blue sky and lightning darts played around the hilltop. Puf! Huntka was carried away by the strong wind, high, high into the angry sky. He was thrown far and fast into space. His two long braids of black hair streamed behind, his loose shirt and fringed leggings, too, caught fire from the lightning. Brilliantly they burned in red, blue, and yellow flames across the sky.

The boy's father, watching from afar, within his teepee, had seen only the black cloud that fell from the clear sky upon the hilltop. He jumped with a start as he saw the zigzag lightnings, and again in another instant the cloud was gone. His heart beat hard. He knew intuitively that some punishment had been sent upon the boy playing with sacred magic. "Alas! Huntka, in his impatience to try the magic, has forgot some of the sacred ceremony! Oh, my heedless, thoughtless boy!" he muttered to himself.

Gathering his robe about his lithe figure, he took long strides toward the hill. As he approached, he saw a great herd of buffalo running about and sniffing the air restlessly. They seemed not to know where to run. They bellowed deep and low, ending with a high shrill note, like the sharp point on their thick horns. Tossing their shaggy heads, they sniffled the airy trail left behind by Huntka as he shot flaming red, blue, and yellow into space.

The father found the smoldering ceremonial fire left by Huntka. The sacred medicine pouch was cast upon the ground! Silent tears trickled down the old medicine man's cheek. He stood lonely upon the hilltop. The constant bellowing of the buffalo herd again attracted him. Following their strange uplifted heads, snorting and tossing their black horns, he looked up into the sky, not knowing where to seek his boy. There across the sky, he saw the first rainbow!

Bidding the buffalo to go their way, he stared at the fabled trail, the invisible path of the great white owl of the North country. Now it was flaming with color! At once he decided to follow the rainbow to its end. He found there his son lying prostrate upon the ground. The boy was no longer like his former self. He lay in a heap, more dead than alive. Had not his father the keen eyes of a medicine man, he would never have recognized his son.

The great medicine man brought forth his most powerful magic. He quickly made a small tent of bent willows. Four stones, heated red hot, he rolled into the enclosure. He sprinkled them with a sacred concoction of herbs. A perfumed vapor filled the lodge. Tenderly carrying the boy in his arms, he thrust him into this medicine lodge.

He awaited the working of this life restoring medicine.

Presently he heard great noises within the lodge. Sounds of horrible, coarse laughter issued from the willow tent. His heart beat hard and loud.

The lodge burst open. A bird, of blackest black, laughing harshly and then screaming, flew away into the far North country.

The boy whose burning shirt and leggings gave color to the rainbow, himself became a black screaming loon.

The Stone Boy
and the Grizzly

The story of the Stone Boy is told widely among the peoples of the Sioux Nation. For example, two versions, told by George Sword and Bad Wound, are collected in James R. Walker's Lakota Myth *(89–100, 141–53). A version by Henry Crow Dog appears in Richard Erdoes and Alfonso Ortiz's* American Indian Myths and Legends *(15–19). Charles Eastman tells the story in* Indian Boyhood, *and Ella Deloria gives a Dakota language, literal translation, and a free translation in* Dakota Texts. *Julian Rice offers a linguistic reading of Deloria's version in* Deer Women and Elk Men. *For an in-depth analysis of this tale, see Elaine Jahner's "Stone Boy: Persistent Hero."*

The thunder spirits had great power (wakan), but conversely, Stone Boy uses his powers to help the four brothers, who turn out to be thunder people. Note also the frequency of the number four in imagery and structure.

One of the longest stories in the collection, this one has several episodes wherein the Stone Boy transforms from stone into human and performs heroic feats. His ability to transform allows him to rescue his friends, defeat his evil mother-in-law (reinforcing kinship taboos), and associate with other larger-than-life heroes. Zitkala-Ša's insertion of the musical score reminds the reader of the oral nature of this tale and that traditional storytelling occurs within a specific cultural and social context. She frames this tale with reference to the Bible, legitimizing the Sioux worldview by comparing the story to the sacred literature of her audience.

Like Moses smiting water out of a rock, the Indian brought forth this story of a nation from the Black rock on the hill side.

In a grass lodge in the middle of the earth a woman lived all alone. Her brothers had gone to hunt the buffaloes and no one of them came back.

There were no people in that country and the woman was very lonely. She often prayed to the thunder spirits that they would send at least some very old person to live with her. At last after she had made many prayers and burned much sweet grass, the wakan people took pity on her. They sent a child. In this manner it happened. At one side of the woman's lodge there was a black stone lying on floor. On this stone she sharpened her knives for the cutting of meat and the tanning of skins. One morning she awoke and this large black stone was gone. Within the hollow of earth where the stone was bedded a babe was lying up on a wild cat's skin.

The woman cried with joy. The child was a fine boy who never fretted nor troubled her. The foster mother cared for this babe tenderly, hunting the best of fruits and cooking soups of sweet roots. Thus the child grew and was able to walk and speak. The mother made many playthings for her foster son and at last a bow and arrows. The Stone Boy soon became expert with his weapons. Before he had seen fifteen winters he became a hunter and was able to furnish meat and skins for the lodge. This boy had often heard his mother speak about her four brothers who had gone to the hunt one morning and had never returned. One brother had gone to the north, one to the east, one to the south, and a fourth to the west, yet no one of them had returned. This was very mysterious.

When the Stone Boy had seen fifteen snows, he wished to go out into the world where people lived.

"Mother," he said, "I wish to go on a journey upon the earth. I will go in a wide circle and it may be that I shall find your brothers who are lost."

The mother dared not refuse her consent because of the mysterious birth of her foster son. So the Stone Boy traveled upon the earth. He walked for many days, going in a wide and constantly decreasing circle until he returned to the lodge of his mother.

He had seen a great many people and had learned a great many things. He had seen men smoking and he wished for a pipe and tobacco.

The mother said, "My son, you must go to the south of here where you will find a quarry of red stone. Fetch hither a piece of this stone and I will fashion a pipe for you." She made for him a tobacco pouch of mole skin. The Stone Boy then went forth seeking the red pipe stone. Though he searched diligently, for a long time he found only one small piece. While he was still looking for the red quarry, he came face to face with Huti the grizzly bear.

The bear sat upon his haunches and showed his teeth in a wicked grin. "Ho, man creature!" said the bear. "I am very glad to see you. This morning I had the hiccoughs; therefore I knew I should soon find fresh meat to eat."

"Do you intend to tear my flesh?" asked the boy.

"Indeed yes," said Huti, licking his chops.

"Do not try to do so," said the Stone Boy, "and I will furnish you good meat from the hunting."

"Ahhguhr!" growled the bear. "I am too hungry to wait for your hunting." Huti seized the boy with his long forearms, but when he thought to close his jaws upon tender flesh he ground his teeth upon a stone and broke them. He shrank back in amazement to see only a black stone where the boy had been. Suddenly the boy leaped from the stone and fell upon the grass, shouting and kicking his heels with laughter.

The grizzly again seized the lad in a rage and broke all his teeth grinding upon a stone. "Now it is my turn," said the Stone Boy as Huti retired in pain and amazement. The boy fitted an arrow to his bow and shot the bear. He killed the grizzly and passed on.[1]

He walked to the top of a hill and saw a very beautiful country, a clear lake with islands surrounded by a pretty wood. While standing upon a hill he heard a man groaning. "Eh-he-o-o-o-n!" moaned the man.

The voice appeared to come from below, and the boy looked downward to some trees. In the crotch of one of these trees he saw a man sitting. The man had no legs. The Stone Boy approached this stranger, who was an aged person, and asked why he had found him thus helpless.

"Alas, grandson," said the old man, "I am suffering because of one man who has destroyed all the people of this very country, killing them with a very long knife. This man cut off my legs and placed me here."

The Stone Boy took this old man down from his perch and carried him to the top of the hill. "My grandson," said the man, "you are very kind. Listen, I am old and wise. Do not go near the first island which you see in yonder lake. There the man lives of whom I have told you. He is of the wakan people and will do you a mischief."

The Stone Boy said, "Very well, grandfather, we shall see about this." He made a sweat lodge and then ran to where he had killed Huti. He cut off the bear's legs and fetched them. He tied these legs to the man's stumps, and so put him in the sweat lodge. He gave the man a vapor bath and then brought him forth. The stranger was half bear and half man.

"Pshaw!" said the boy. "This is indeed a poor creature!" He seized the man by his bear's legs and swung him to and fro, tossing him into some tall grass.

"You shall be a brown bear like no other," said the boy. As he said this a brown bear came from the grass and fled into some woods. Since then there have been brown bears on the earth.

The Stone Boy was now very curious about the mysterious island and the wakan man of whom he had heard. He went to the island, swimming a neck of the lake. When he had arrived he soon discovered the tepee of the wakan man. This lodge was of birch bark and was surrounded by a defense of posts covered with bark. The Stone Boy picked up a pebble and cast it hard against the tepee.

Immediately an old man came out and ran around the lodge, looking hither and thither. The boy became a stone and the wakan man could not see him. Three times the boy cast a pebble against the tepee, and three times the old man ran out to see whither the missile had come. At last the Stone Boy leaped the stockade and followed the wakan man into his lodge. The old man sat at the back of his tepee, his knees raised high and clasping either leg with a hand. Inside his lodge poles were hung with wotawe (powerful "medicine" charms) which would protect the body of the wearer from harm. Near the lodge door there hung a strange appearing drum and a lance.

For a long time the old man sat in silence looking steadily at the Stone Boy. He smoked a pipe, the bowl of which was made of the trunk ribs of a human skeleton. He knew this boy was wakan. When night came on the two lay upon some skins and slept without having spoken.

In the morning the old man arose. He cooked papa and wasna. "Get up grandson and eat meat," he said.

When they had eaten, the Stone Boy said, "Grandfather, I wish you would make me some arrows."

"Very well," said the wakan man. "Go out and cut some sticks of the Juneberry trees. Go across to the mainland."

The boy went, and while he was cutting rods among the Juneberries, five young women carrying bags passed by, following a path. Behind these girls the Stone Boy heard the music of flute and song. This is the song which four young men were singing.

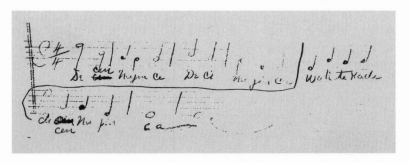

Score sung by four young men in the tale "The Stone boy and the Grizzly." Gertrude and Raymond Bonnin Collection [MSS 1704]. Courtesy of L. Tom Perry Special Collections, Harold B. Lee Library, Brigham Young University, Provo, Utah.

The young men who sang were walking behind the young women. They were courting these girls, whom they wished to marry.

One of these young men saw the Stone Boy. "He-e-e!" he called. "Come on and go with us."

"What are you going to do?" asked the boy.

"We are going to court those handsome girls whom you saw. Come and assist us with music."

"Wait and I will do so," said the Stone Boy. He ran to the tepee of the wakan man, crossing the shallow water by jumping from stone to stone.

"Grandfather," he cried, "some young men are going to court some girls and I wish to go with them."

"Do so," said the old man. "See, here are many things that are sacred, charms which will assist you in any undertaking. Choose ye among them, but do not take the lance and drum which are my own wotawe."[2]

The Stone Boy dressed himself in some very fine skins. He painted his face and put bear's oil on his hair. Having made himself ready, he suddenly cut the strings of the sacred drum and lance and darted out of the lodge.

"H-e-e-e!" cried the wakan man. "What have you done? Bring back my lance and drum."

He ran after the boy but could not catch him. Again he called to the boy, "H-e-e-e! Grandson, stop, I wish to speak with you." The Stone Boy halted, laughing. "Grandson," said the old man, "I see that you are very bold. You fear nothing. Therefore, take my drum and lance, and here are some sacred charms to go with them."

He gave the boy some medicine powder to blow upon his breast and a charm to put in his mouth. "You must be careful in using the drum," said the wakan man. "You must never beat this drum very hard, for its rattle reaches to the upper world and causes a great wind to blow which will destroy everything."

"Good," said the Stone Boy. "I will indeed remember what you have said."

46

The boy now crossed the water and followed after the four young men. Presently he overtook them. Together they traveled until the sun sank beneath the earth. They came to the tepee of the young women. Near to this they camped to eat and rest. The four young men belonged to the thunder people, and they supposed that the Stone Boy was not wakan, as they were, but like other men.

The eldest now spoke to his younger brother. "Misun," he said, "we are in need of something to eat; therefore, do you and this stranger go out and kill some animal."

The younger and the Stone Boy went to some woods and very soon they killed a cow elk. When they had returned with the meat, the eldest said to the Stone Boy: "Now, koda, do you go to the tepee of those girls and borrow a kettle in which to cook our meat."[3]

So the Stone Boy went to the tepee of the young women. They said, "Yes, you shall have a pot of rawhide, but in return, see that you come back and entertain us with music."

When the boy had returned to his fellows, they made a feast. While their meat was cooking, the four burned sweet grass and produced their wotawe (medicine charms) praying the Great Mystery to bless them in their undertaking.

They sang a chant, laying their medicine bags in row, "Ate, ma yu ju ju wo, cepaya ma yu ju ju wo," which interpreted, "Father untie me, father untie me with prayers."

While they were singing this chant, they untied their medicine bags and laid them in a row. The Stone Boy sat looking on. He was not invited to take part in their sacred ceremonies, for he was regarded as merely a person of the under world or earth world.

The Stone Boy was very hungry and wished to eat meat, but when they had finished their prayers the eldest of the brothers said to him, "Friend, you may not eat with men of our sort, so while we are feasting you had better take your robe and lie down in some secret place."

The boy took his robe and lay down behind a tree. He did

not like to do so, for he was very hungry. Then the brothers began their feast. While they were eating a storm arose, as was usual with thunder people, and wind, fire, and hail fell upon the earth, making the trees to roar and the ground to quake. When these thunder people had finished, the storm ceased.

There was little meat left for the Stone Boy when he arose from his couch. "Now it is my time to eat," said the boy. He came forward with his drum and lance.

The four brothers nudged each other with their elbows and laughed. "What will this one find to eat?" they whispered. "Lo, this fellow is only a man."

"Now friends," said the Stone Boy, "I make myself a feast, therefore I advise you to cover yourselves well."

The young men laughed. They covered their heads with skins. "Let us see what this boy will do," they said.

The Stone Boy gathered the remnants of meat and set the borrowed pot before him. Then he beat his drum, and lo, a noise of deep thunder immediately shook the earth and rolled upward to the sky. A wind arose with cracking thunder and zigzag lightning, so that nothing had been seen or heard on the earth like to this.

The Stone Boy began eating while branches of trees were falling all about. The four brothers were scared. They saw that this boy was indeed wakan and very powerful. The wind hurled them against trees, where they clung, crying out to the Stone Boy to hasten his eating. "We do not wish to be destroyed!" cried the brothers. The boy continued to eat calmly and slowly, and the wind blew harder, tearing trees from the earth. But when he had finished eating, the storm subsided and no one had been destroyed.

The Stone Boy now carried their raw hide kettle back to the young women. "Presently," he said, "we will come and talk with you."

The young men smoked their pipes, then all went to visit the young women. They danced and sang, displaying their fine clothes and decorations. So they visited, courting the girls for a time, then returned to their camp fire and slept.

In the morning when they awoke, they were very cold, for the young women had stolen their leggings and robes and were gone.

"Now what shall we do about this?" they asked each other as they warmed their naked limbs at a fire. When they had eaten meat, one said, "Come, let us follow these girls and secure them for our wives."

So they took the trail of the five young women. After a time they came to a large grass lodge strongly fortified. In this sacred lodge dwelt the five young women and their mother, who was a witch and wife to the wakan man of the mysterious island.

Into the lodge of these women the young men knew they would not be permitted to enter, unless by stealth or force.

They stood without, considering for a time. Then each produced his sacred charms and prayed to the spirit of thunders, looking aloft and closing his eyes. Then one by one they approached to break down the stockade and enter the sacred lodge by force.

But each time one seized upon the defense, an old woman appeared and threw a powder upon him. Each time she came out of the lodge to cast her powder, a man fell and lay upon his back, motionless as the dead.

The Stone Boy only was left unharmed. He paid no attention to this old woman. He put his drum behind him and walked toward the lodge enclosure. As he came near, the old woman came forth and threw her powder at him. The Stone Boy suddenly swung his drum in front, and the woman was powerless to do him harm.

"He-he-he!" cried the witch woman. "Now indeed is my husband Witko (silly), for having given his magic drum to this boy. Lo, we shall be undone!"

The Stone Boy walked into the tepee where her daughters were. "Now," said he, "return the clothing you have taken and build a sweat lodge for these men who are ill. They shall indeed be your husbands."

The young women did as he bade them. He had overcome

the witch woman, their mother; therefore they hastened to do his bidding. When the young men were cured of their fainting, the Stone Boy said to them, "Choose ye your wives, and do not any longer trifle with sacred things. I will attend to all these things. I also will hunt meat for our families."

On the following morning the old woman said to her sons-in-law, "Lo, my sons, arise quickly, for I have seen an elk which I wish you to kill. This bull elk is gone to a brook near at hand."

The young men arose and took their weapons, but the Stone Boy cried out to them that they should stay in the lodge. "I, myself, will kill this elk," he said. But the men would not listen. They were hungry and they hastily took their weapons and went forth.

The Stone Boy passed out of the lodge and went far around and hid himself behind a dead tree. Soon he saw a bull elk coming up from the brook. As this elk came walking, smoke issued from his nostrils and flint arrow teeth were hurled from his mouth. These flint stones flew like real arrows, cutting bushes and tree branches and making a rattling noise like the pelting of hail upon dry leaves. The Stone Boy's brothers were wounded by these arrows, and each man fell to the earth.

When the elk saw these men fall he stopped and rolled his eyes about wickedly. "I thought my mother said there were five of these simpletons," he said. This elk was the witch woman's powerful son.

The Stone Boy now stepped from behind his tree and launched an arrow into the wicked one. The elk fell with a bellow of pain, shooting his flint stones, and the Stone Boy escaped as before. Presently the women came out from their lodge and approached. When they saw the fallen hunters, they all laughed. "But I do not see this Stone Boy fallen," said the old woman. "My son should have killed him also."

The Stone Boy stepped out from hiding. "Mother-in-law," he said, "here is a bull elk which I have killed. Hurry up and cut up the meat for I am hungry."

"Him na him!" cried the old woman. 4 "Alas, alas, my son is dead."

"Now," said the Stone Boy to the wives, "put your husbands in a sweat lodge and give them life and strength to recover."

The wives dared not disobey, and presently the wounded ones recovered from their hurts.

After many moons, the witch woman arose early one morning and went forth from the lodge. When she returned, she said, "Sons-in-law, I have discovered some strange creature hiding beneath an earth bank. Do come out and see what it is."

"Lie in your blankets," said the Stone Boy. "Hitherto you have caused me enough of trouble." So the brothers remained in the lodge and the Stone Boy went forth.

"Come on, mother-in-law," said the boy. "You must come and show me this creature."

"No, but you go on," urged the old woman. "What I have seen is near by under the high earth bank."

The Stone Boy seized the witch woman and pushed her before him. When they had come to the earth bank, lo, Unkte-hi, the water monster, lay in the water with mouth agape.

Suddenly the old woman attempted to push the Stone Boy over the bank. They struggled fiercely, pushing each other to and fro. The witch woman was very strong. She shouted her war cry, deeming to gain the victory, but found herself very suddenly pushing at a large black stone.

She attempted to heave this rock into the water when the earth gave way under her feet. She fell into the mouth of Unk-tehi and was destroyed.

The Stone Boy returned to the lodge. He said to his brothers, "Come now, it appears that we have lived long enough at this place. You can go forth and take care of yourselves. I shall return to visit my father-in-law."

The Stone Boy commanded his wife to make a bundle of her clothing. Together they went into the woods. As they were walking, the wife said, "Husband, you must make a sacred feast for your grandfather. He is my father, but he is very wicked and I fear him. It would be much better if he were dead. He does not eat the red beaver, for when he eats of its meat some dreadful thing will happen to him. He is bound to eat of your sacred feast, therefore kill a red beaver and disguise the flesh until he shall have eaten."

The Stone Boy went into a bog land and tread about heavily, shaking the earth. Presently a red beaver came out of the water and the boy shot it. His wife dressed the meat, and they carried it with them to the lodge of her father.

"Father-in-law, you see I have married your daughter and am returned. I shall make a sacred feast for you."

"How, how, do so my son," said this old man. So the woman cooked meat and they smoked sacred tobacco and burned sweet grass, making prayers.

"Now father-in-law," said the Stone Boy, when they had finished this business, "I invite you to the wakan wohanpi (sacred feast). Let us smoke and make an offering."

So they again burned sweet grass and laid their medicine bags in a row, blowing the sweet smelling smoke upon them, and singing the sacred chants.

They sat down to the feast and the old man took meat and smelled of it. "How, my son," he said. "I do not eat the meat of the red beaver."

"But you can not refuse," said the Stone Boy. "At any rate, you must take some of the soup."

The wicked old man hesitated. He rolled his eyes about and his limbs trembled. But he dared not refuse to partake of a sacred feast. So he drank a little of the soup and tasted meat. Then he excused himself. He mentioned all his relatives, saying that these should take his place at this feast and for their sake he had refrained from further eating. He also muttered prayers to protect himself and lit his sacred pipe, blowing a great deal of smoke through his nostrils.

The man's medicine did not protect him. He became very ill and lay upon the ground groaning. "Alas, alas, my drum and lance!" he muttered.

He continued very ill, and, in the night, the Stone Boy awoke to find himself adrip with sweat and half dead from suffocation. He uncovered his head and saw that the wakan man was become like a huge toad, having swollen until his body filled the lodge and his skin was stretched as the rawhide upon a drum's head.

The Stone Boy's wife had gone outside the lodge. "Come," she said to her husband. "My father will burst and harm will befall us." So the two went away into a wood. As they were walking they heard a sound as of thunder, a deep mutter which rolled through the woods, shaking the earth.

In the morning the husband and wife returned to the lodge of the wakan man. The lodge was destroyed and the old man lay upon the ground broken in pieces.

"Drag this body into the water, husband," said the Stone Boy's wife. The Stone Boy did so. The body lay upon the water all night, and in the morning the head and back of a great fish appeared.

"Soon this man will be all fish," said the Stone Boy. At midday it was so. A very large fish raised part way out of the water and dived beneath the surface. Thus the wakan man became the chief of fishes.

"Let us now go to my mother" said the Stone Boy. "It appears that a hundred winters have passed since I lived with her."

They traveled over the hills, and a son was born to them during the journey. When they had arrived at the place where the Stone Boy's mother had dwelt, her tepee was gone. There was no trace of the woman.

The Stone Boy and his wife went northward toward a stream, and after a time they met a bent old woman carrying a bag of artichokes.

"Lo, this is my mother," said the Stone Boy. He spoke to her. "Ina," he said, "I have returned to you, bringing my wife and child."

The woman cried out with disbelief, until she saw a black stone where the boy had stood. Then she cried with great joy.

The Stone Boy now hunted for his family. He took much

meat and many skins and his wife dressed some very fine hides and made a large tepee, so that they dwelt very well on the earth.

One day four men and their families suddenly appeared. These were the brothers with their wives and children.

"Behold," they said, "we are of the thunder people. Since parting with you we have visited our sky world and there we learned that the Stone Boy was indeed our nephew, born in the tepee of our sister. We have heard that our nephew and brother will become the father of a great nation and that many tribes will come shortly to destroy him. Thus we are come to war against his enemy."

The Stone Boy and his brothers now made many arrows and war weapons. Soon there was need to use them, for there came vast armies of flies and mosquitoes and of all evil tribes which dwell upon the earth. All creatures of the woods and upper air sought to destroy men that there should be none henceforth upon the earth. The five men fought with these tribes and overcame them. So it is that man may dwell upon the earth.

The Stone Boy and his relatives became a great nation. After a great many moons they removed to a country of hills and pitched their tepees. When they had done this the Stone Boy retired to the top of a high hill, where he sat for a long time in meditation. His wife came to him to know his will. The Stone Boy said to her, "Go back, and in four days, return bringing all our people to look upon me."

The woman returned to the village, and in four days the people followed her back to her husband. Upon the hill where the Stone Boy had sat they saw nothing but a large black stone.

The Making of Thunder People

This story introduces Wakinyan, *the thunderbird. In conjunction with the* Wakantanka *(the great mystery; all powers, spiritual beings, creation of all things), the thunderbird is the source of the speaking thunder and central to Sioux traditions.*

Like the other longer and episodic stories, characters that appear early and seem important disappear as the hero/main character faces various challenges. The transformation of Tahince-Iheya from mortal to thunder deity requires many trials and tests. Again a character named Huntka appears, but here it is as a wicked female and a gull, not as a male loon. Like other stories, this tale has recurrent emphasis on the number four but also introduces symbolic colors of yellow and blue. This is one of the few stories that is dated—"April 17, 1906" is handwritten in the title page.

Four brothers lived together in one tepee. They had no parents living nor any relatives near of kin. The three oldest were hunters. The youngest was a lad of but few winters. Having no mother to make for him proper clothing, he wore a hood continually. At first the garment was too large, but as the boy grew his head filled the beaded hood to bursting. Thus he went around with his ears sticking out of this old hood.

The name of this boy was Tahince-Iheya.[1]

So these brothers lived thus for a long time, until a strange woman, passing that way, stopped at their tepee, saying that she had come to keep house for them. The brothers adopted this woman as their sister. She was called Huntka, The Gull, and she did very well, performing all the labor at home while the elder brothers attended to their hunting.

After they had lived thus for twelve moons, the elder

brothers went out one morning as usual to hunt. During the day there was a great deal of thunder, and Tahince-Iheya and his sister Huntka saw a black cloud of smoke above some trees in the distance. They were afraid of this cloud, and so hid themselves in the tepee. That night the elder brothers did not return. They came no more to their former lodge.

So it was that Huntka and the boy Tahince-Iheya lived alone. They were very hungry at times, until the moon of ripe plums came. Each morning Huntka went out after plums. She bade her brother to stay at home and look after the teepee. At first Huntka stayed in the woods but little time and returned, fetching her parfleche filled with fine plums. But soon the woman began to stay out all day, and at night she brought but few plums and these were not good.

Each morning Huntka would say: "Younger brother, I must go further in search of the plums. Fear nothing therefore if I do not return until late."

Still the woman brought no more good plums. Tahince-Iheya began to question himself: "Why does my sister make herself so much trouble? I will see about this."

Secretly he had been going out and snaring rabbits for his eating, so he was no longer afraid to go in the woods. His sister arose early and went out as usual. In a little time Tahince-Iheya followed her. Huntka went far through the bush and woodlands until she stood upon a hill in an open country. Tahince-Iheya watched from the cover of the bushes. Presently he saw a black cloud descend from the sky and cover the hill. Huntka was swallowed up in this cloud. Tahince-Iheya heard the voice of a thunder-person speaking in this cloud, and also saw his zigzag red arrows flying athwart the hill.

"Oh-ho!" said Tahince-Iheya. "It is indeed thus." He returned to his tepee.

When the snows came, Tahince-Iheya said to his sister: "Do not now go forth any more from the tepee. I myself have become a hunter and will see that you are provided."

He went to the woods and took many rabbits, and the woman was sustained.

When the moon of tall grass came, a child was born in the tepee. It was a boy.

"I think he will indeed be a great fellow," said Tahince-Iheya. "Now therefore, I name him Hupuhu-sda." This name signifies Rattling Wings.

Huntka and her brother lived for two more winters, and the child grew to walk about the tepee. This boy, Rattling Wings, was a very fine child, and his uncle, Tahince-Iheya, loved him.

One morning Huntka said, "See after your nephew, younger brother; I am going for some wood."

The woman went out but did not return. That night Tahince-Iheya had much trouble to do for the child, which cried for its mother. In the morning he said, "I will go and look for my sister at that place."

He took his nephew upon his back and went to the hill of thunders. There he waited till the sun hid, going into the earth, but he saw nothing of his sister. He carried his nephew home, and again the child cried.

In the night thunder people arrived, making a great uproar overhead, and much rain fell. During this rain a man suddenly entered at the tepee door. Lightnings came with him, and Tahince-Iheya saw that he was a very tall warrior, and bore arms.

"How," said Tahince-Iheya. "Who are you that enters my tepee?"

"Brother-in-law," said the stranger, "I am come for my son. I fear indeed that he is giving you much trouble. You wish also to find your sister. To-morrow you will travel for one sun to the southwest until you shall come to a village, where you will find Huntka, who is married to a chief's son. I will now take your nephew with me."

Tahince-Iheya embraced his nephew and the man took the child away.

On the following morning, Tahince-Iheya went forth from his tepee. He traveled all day to the south-west. At night he arrived at a village. He was very tired and hungry, but he saw some boys playing at hoop and sticks, and he stopped to watch their game.

"He-e-e! Tahince-Iheya!" cried these boys. They seemed to know him and were pleased at his coming. As Tahince-Iheya stood leaning upon a stick, he saw his sister coming out to him. "How, how, Sister!" he cried. He was very glad.

"Why do you call me Sister?" asked the woman angrily. She attacked him with a staff, beating him over the head.

The boys who were playing hoops and sticks shouted at the woman: "He-hee! Why do you abuse so small a boy?" They ran at the woman and drove her away with their sticks.

An old woman who lived in a smoky tepee now came and led Tahince-Iheya away. This old woman took the lad to her lodge, where she put herbs on his head and said medicine prayers for the cure of his hurts.

In the morning Huntka came across the tribal circle, carrying an old shin bone. She threw this bone into the tepee of the old woman. "Tahince," she said, "eat your bone and then go with your brother-in-law to the hunt. Whatsoever he shall kill, that you shall carry home."

So Tahince-Iheya ate meat from the bone, and followed his brother-in-law to the hunt. The man traveled far in the woods, saying nothing; then he killed an elk. Although this hunter feared his mysterious wife, he had a kind heart. He carried the elk's meat to within a very little distance of home. And then put it upon Tahince-Iheya's shoulders. Thus was the day's kill carried home always, until the wicked one suspected.

One day Huntka secretly followed the hunters. Her husband suspected this, and when he had killed a deer, he tied the legs with an arrow string and strung the carcass upon the boy's shoulder. Thus Tahince-Iheya walked homeward with the arrow string cutting his flesh. The woman was satisfied.

That night Wakinyan, Chief of the Thunder People, came to Tahince-Iheya in a dream.

"Natala (Nephew)," said Wakinyan, "I am your real brother-in-law and your sister is become a wicked woman by this last marriage. Little brother, to-morrow when Huntka's husband goes to the hunt, do you go with him as you have done regularly. When he kills an elk, tell him you wish to eat the heart. He will give you the heart. Take your time and roast it well. When you have eaten, a cloud will appear overhead. I will be in the cloud. When you shall hear my voice in the thunder, you must run very quickly and take refuge under a birch tree."

So, the next day they went hunting, and again the man killed an elk. "Brother-in-law," said Tahince-Iheya, "I wish to dress this elk and cook the heart for my eating."

"Hurry up about it, then," said the man, "lest your sister arrive before you have finished."

But the boy worked very leisurely. He roasted the heart well and ate slowly. When he had finished eating, lo, a black cloud appeared flying above the trees. Out of this cloud the red arrows of the thunder people were shot against all the woods.

Tahince-Iheya ran quickly to the shelter of the birch tree. The thunder people cannot hit these trees. While the boy stood, thunder voices rattled, the beating of the wings of Wakinyan, until his ears were bursting. When the voices ceased, Tahince-Iheya indeed saw Wakinyan standing by a pine tree. Suddenly this tree dropped into the earth, smoking.

Wakinyan now spoke to the boy. "Go back to the village," he said, "and see where is now that wicked woman, your sister."

So the boy returned, and lo, the village was burned, and its people were destroyed. Only the smoky tepee of the old woman had escaped.

Again Wakinyan appeared to the boy. "Will you now go with me?" asked the thunder spirit. "Or do you choose to stay on the earth?"

"I will go with you," said Tahince-Iheya.

So his brother-in-law took him into a wood and said, "Come hither aside and see what will happen. You are now about to leave the earth, and you have no friends of your own people to note your passing or to mourn your departure. But there are other people who will wish to speak with you. I will make myself invisible, for these people cannot look upon me and live."

Wakinyan vanished, and Tahince-Iheya stood alone.

Presently he heard many foot falls and saw the tops of bushes waving, and there appeared a bull moose, a bear, and a cougar, who came and stood before him.

"How, Tahince-Iheya," said these, "we await the arrival of others."

A deer, a wolf, an eagle, and a lynx came.

"How, Tahince-Iheya," said these, "others will come after us."

Thus arrived a mouse, a rabbit, a snake, and a fish-hawk, and after these many folk of different tribes. It appeared that each tribe sent one person. When they were all assembled in a tribal circle, the bear addressed the boy.

"Ho, Tahince-Iheya," said the bear. "We have heard that you are to go upward to the country of Thunders and Whirlwinds. We desire therefore that you shall speak to Wakinyan, chief of the thunder people. Therefore we shall pass before you, each making his prayer."

And this was done. Each one as he passed before Tahince-Iheya stopped and made a present of beads. Each one gave beads of a different color and made his prayer thus:

"Wakinyan, Wakinyan hear me, pity me! You are very powerful. Keep my feet from forbidden ways, that the red arrows of the thunders may be turned aside."

Thus saying, they went away into the woods. Again Wakinyan appeared to Tahince-Iheya. He took the boy upon his back. "Shut your eyes," he commanded. "We will now go upward through a hole in the sky. Four times you will feel something touch you under the arm pit. At the fourth time, we shall arrive at my world."

Suddenly Tahince-Iheya felt himself borne aloft. Something touched him with a sharp pain under the arm, and again a second time. The boy was very curious, feeling himself thus airily soaring upward. He disobeyed his brother-in-law and opened his eyes. Suddenly he fell through space and the thunder-spirit dove beneath and caught him.

"How is this!" said Wakinyan. "This will not do; you must keep your eyes shut."

The boy obeyed, keeping his eyes closed until the pain had touched him four times and they were arrived among the thunder people.

Here Tahince-Iheya saw a strange folk in a strange world. These people were indeed the thunder spirits. They lived in a beautiful village, with four courts, on an open plain, with woods on one side. These strange ones mostly sat about in front of their tepees smoking long pipes with curiously carved bowls of blue pipe-stone.

Wakinyan led the way to his own tepee. Here Tahince-Iheya saw his nephew, Hupuhu-sda. This boy sat upon the ground opposite the tepee door. He held a spear in one hand and a large war club in the other. He had become very great. Tahince-Iheya desired, indeed, to become like him.

The boy from the under-world thus saw himself alone—a human creature among all these thunder people, who ate their meat raw and were able to do mysterious things.

Tahince-Iheya lived with his Wakan brother-in-law and nephew. Every morning he went to the wood and shot pigeons, which he cooked and ate by himself. One day as he was hunting and shot his arrow at a pigeon, the shaft alighted in a spring of muddy water. He approached this spring to get his weapon and his feet sunk in a yellow mire. He saw water boiling and bubbling in the spring. This was also yellow. He seized his arrow and struggled out of the mud.

When he had done this, Tahince-Iheya returned to the village of the thunder people. When the people saw him, they became very much excited. They pointed their fingers at him and whistled: "Phee-u-u! Whee-u-u!"

"What have I done indeed? What has gone wrong with me?" Tahince-Iheya questioned himself. He went to his brother-in-law's tepee, and the people came and peered in at him with continued excitement. They pointed their fingers, and their shrill whistling bit the ears. Tahince-Iheya felt very much embarrassed.

Then his nephew, Rattling Wings, spoke to him: "You must tell very quickly what you have seen," he said. "What has happened to you? These people are indeed very curious to know."

"I should think so," said Tahince-Iheya. "It is nothing, however. I merely shot my arrow into a yellow spring. I ran to get it, and got my leggings muddy. This is a little matter for so much fuss."

This reply excited the thunder people still further. They ran hither and thither, cracking the joints of their wings, which emitted flashes of lightning. They doubled themselves upon their thighs, gesticulating and making strange noises.

"Uncle," said Rattling Wings, "this is no small matter. You have indeed found something dreadful. You have discovered the dwelling of our enemy, Unktehi. Heretofore we have not known where this underwater monster lived. You have done well. To-morrow we shall go and kill this Unktehi."

So, on the morrow Tahince-Iheya guided the thunder folk to the spring of yellow waters. The people surrounded this spring and attacked the waters with lightnings. The spring was troubled. Spouts and jets of muddy water were thrown upward, and the ground shook under their feet.

Unktehi refused to come to the surface. Thus failing to see the enemy, Rattling Wings rose in the air above the dwelling of Unktehi and poised his spear. Lightnings darted from his spear point into the boiling water with much cracking of thunder. Unktehi came to the surface, making the mud fly. Thus the monster floundered, making a great uproar until he was dead.

The people rejoiced greatly. They drew Unktehi out of his muddy waters and cut up his body and ate his flesh raw.

When Hupuhu-sda, or Rattling Wings, saw this, he became anxious about his uncle.

"Behold," he said, "what shall this human one do among us? He will be regularly getting into trouble. He may even be killed. Therefore, let us make him one of us."

"Do so if you can," said his father. "You are very powerful among the Wakan people!"

So Hupuhu-sda asked his uncle to go with him to a wood at some distance. They went and saw a ground very rough with stones and the trunks of gnarled old trees. Here the thunder birds had their nests. There were many nests, having different colored eggs—white, blue, red, and yellow.

"Lo, now you are Tahince-Iheya, a human person," said Hupuhu-sda, "and we wish to make you a thunder person. Which of these eggs, Uncle, do you wish that I shall put you in?"

"Put me in this huge, white egg in the blue nest," said Tahince-Iheya, who indeed wished to become Wakinyan. And Hupuhu-sda caused him to go into the egg.

"I will return in four days," said Hupuhu-sda. In four days he came. The egg was grown very large, filling all the nest, and its shell was cracked in places. Again he went away and returned in four days. The shell of the egg was now fallen to pieces, and the mysterious new one lifted its beak.

Again Hupuhu-sda went home, and returned in four days. A thunder being was in the blue nest—a very great mysterious one was growing. This one had no wings as yet, but lightnings were playing about all his joints and thunder voices muttered shaking the feet.

"Truly, this is a terrible fellow already," said Hupuhu-sda. "He makes me to fear. Be careful how you move, Uncle," he said, "lest some harm befall."

A fourth time Hupuhu-sda returned to the village of the thunder people. He told these people of the wonderful, mysterious one, new-born of thunders.

"This new one will soon appear among us," said Hupuhu-sda. "He will come with great lightnings and a great wind. Therefore, drive fast all your tepee stakes lest this village be destroyed. Also we must pray to Tahince-Iheya," he said. "Therefore make your pipes ready."

He went again to his uncle, but dared not approach near to him, for a whirl-wind was circling about and clouds hovered above the nest of the thunder-bird.

"Be careful, Uncle, how you approach the village!" shouted Hupuhu-sda. "Ho! Ho! Come slowly, that no harm may come to us. You are indeed become very great and powerful."

So Tahince-Iheya moved toward the village, going slowly amid thunders and whirlwinds. The people came forth to meet him. They smoked sacred pipes and prayed to this great, mysterious one. As he approached leisurely, they had much ado to save their village. The wind blew a hurricane and rain fell, flooding the earth.

Thus the great mysterious one arrived and was appeased. So it was that he became Tahince-Iheya: chief of thunder and whirlwind people.

Zicha, the Squirrel, and Iktomi

In this story the squirrel, Zicha (Dakota), represents virtues of generosity, hospitality, and power. The trickster, Iktomi, is the typical bungling host. Zitkala-Ša handwrites at the top of this story, "Iktomi is the spider, personified, appearing like an Indian." Both characters also take on human form. The eating and cooking utensils and the method of cooking reflect early Plains material culture and practices.

Iktomi explicitly demonstrates gluttony, pride, blasphemy, and disrespect for life. His children are also ill mannered. In addition to Iktomi's general rudeness, he violates the sacred by vainly imitating Zicha's powerful rituals. Such a violation inevitably leads to destruction.

Stylistically and in content, this story is most like Zitkala-Ša's stories in Old Indian Legends.

Zicha, the squirrel, and old Iktomi were near neighbors one summer time. Zicha was a clever athlete and hunter. His family never went hungry or a begging.

Iktomi was a real do-nothing and served only in mischief making. Sometimes he did cunning tricks, and then again he would be the most stupid man in camp. No one could depend upon Iktomi, he was so unreliable. It is told his offspring are mean little imps who scratched the children with whom they played, and pulled their hair.

It happened one day when Zicha was hunting that he came close by Iktomi's teepee. He was so tired and hungry that he dropped in. He hoped that Iktomi would be polite enough to share a hot drink of herbs, as was the custom. Or if he had been successful in the hunt, he might even get a nice bowl of soup and tender chunks of boiled meat! Zicha reckoned wrong.

Not by any chance did Iktomi ever have food in his dwelling. It was a mystery how he reared his family. Likely they made their daily rounds of calls upon their neighbors and lived off their hospitality.

There was no food in Iktomi's tent. Zicha saw in a moment he must go on home without luncheon. The peaked faces of the lean and hungry Iktomi children impressed him. He rose to depart. "Come with your family tomorrow and dine at my teepee, when the sun is in the zenith," he said.

Iktomi and his unlovely brood arrived early at Zicha's teepee. They were made welcome and seated upon great buffalo robes in the guests' quarter of the teepee circle.

Unused to the ways of real folks, they did not know how to behave in company. The Iktomi children were meddlesome, thievish, and very destructive. It speaks a great deal for Mrs. Zicha's hospitality that she received them at all.

The Iktomi family were hardly seated when the children were up on their feet again. One began tearing the pretty beads loose from the handsome bags against the wall of the teepee. Another was untying the strings that fastened the mouth of the bags, even breaking some of them.

This did not disturb father Iktomi. It was his false notion of being good to his children—to let them do as they pleased. It certainly was not being kind to his friends who had invited them to dine. But that was beyond Iktomi's understanding. Shutting his eyes to the unpardonable pranks of his hateful children, Iktomi sat serenely and talked very loud. The well bred little squirrelly girls looked playfully at the Iktomi girls. They were about to run out doors for games when father Zicha said, "Daughters mine, brush your hair smooth and glossy. Then stand before me." They did as he requested. They were well bred little sisters. With a squinted eye, pretending to be very serious, Zicha asked, "Which one of you girls shall I kill for our dinner?" The Zicha sisters danced up and down, shouting joyously, "Miye! Miye!" (Me! Me! Me!).

Father Zicha had funny little scary games he played with

his children, and they grew to like them. They were such fun!
Today, he chose the youngest daughter and led her out of the
teepee. Presently, they heard him killing something. He came
in carrying a fine fat beaver. His wife cooked it in a rawhide kettle, with hot stones from the center fire. It was ready to serve.

With a buffalo horn ladle, Zicha's wife gave generous help-
ings to the guests. Just before they began eating, Zicha said,
"My friends, do not break any of the joints of the bones. This is
a rule we observe when eating the beaver." Iktomi ate glutto-
nously. He was nearly starved. He really felt like devouring the
whole of the beaver himself, but by superhuman effort he
restrained his huge appetite. He gnawed the bones noisily, rapidly, and exceedingly clean.

His sharp tooth struck the small joint of a fore foot and
broke it.

Iktomi apologized profusely. "He-he-he, I didn't bite hard,
but the joint snapped so easily!" he said, trying to excuse himself for the breach of etiquette.

The smallest Iktomi girl fell into a temper because their
soup bowl grew empty; she kicked right and left and struck out
with both arms. The buffalo horn ladle she held in her hand
she threw across the center fire. It struck the sleeping Zicha
baby full in the face and made it cry.

When the dinner was over, Zicha's eldest daughter gathered all the bones and threw them far out of the teepee door.
Zicha's youngest daughter returned laughing but limping on
one little foot.

Iktomi's mouth fell ajar. His eyes were glued upon the lame
foot. He was trying to put the broken bones together in his
mind, the beaver's foot and the Zicha girl's foot, but he failed
utterly to understand. The secret was too deep for him. He
resumed his smoking with father Zicha. All the while they
talked his eyes continually followed the little lame foot.

Foolish Iktomi, there was certainly a scum over his vision.
He did not know true art when he saw it with wide open eyes.
In his own conceit, he thought himself clever, and crudely imi-

tating heroes and wise men, the blunderhead thought he was one of them!

Taking his leave of Zicha, he invited him with his family to dine! "Come tomorrow noon," Iktomi said. "I shall prepare a feast in royal fashion."

On midday the day following, Zicha and his family called upon the Iktomis. Scarcely were they seated, when Iktomi, itching to perform miracles too, gave a command to his wife. "Heat water in the kettle with the red hot stones. Have boiling water ready," he said, affecting the dignity of a medicine man. To his own daughters he said, "You brush your long hair, smooth and glossy. Then stand before me."

Zicha and his wife looked at each other out of a corner of an eye. Iktomi was repeating the very words he heard Zicha use the previous day. Of course they had no meaning for him. They were sounds. That was all.

The Iktomi girls did not smooth their tangled hair, but stood in front. Out of a bold curiosity, Iktomi growled at them, "Which one of you girls shall I kill for our dinner?" Hereupon they screamed with fright and tore frantically out of the small teepee door. They had never heard their father say such a thing! He chased them, grabbing at them with his long tawny hands. The bad girls ran. They thought their father had suddenly gone crazy. He caught one by the foot and led her away from the teepee. "Rabbit! Rabbit! Hurry! Or Fawn! Fawn! Hurry! Anything for the feast, hurry," Iktomi prayed with his eyes shut. "She will return when the bones are thrown out of the teepee door," he assured himself. He waited for the miracle. Iktomi at length opened his eyes, fully expecting to see in his hand a rabbit or fawn or deer.

Oh, there had been no magic! No miracle! Only there was one less imp of Iktomi among the people, left.

This ended the dinner party. Zicha and his father, on leaving the lodge, again invited Iktomi to dine the following day.

They came early as usual. Iktomi and his family were dressed in mourning, their hair cut squarely at the neck and their faces painted with black paint. Cordially they were received and seated within the teepee circle.

Zicha requested his wife to hang the kettle upon the forked stake, driven aslant over the center fire. He went outside and climbed the teepee. He chirped like a squirrel all the way up till he reached the top of the highest pole. The Iktomis looked up at him through the smoke lapel of the teepee. They saw a squirrel sitting upon the teepee pole. They saw him take out a knife and cut his waist line clear across. Instantly wild rice came pouring down into the kettle of boiling water below.

Zicha came down and dined with his guests upon a dinner of magic rice.

When they had smoked and the visitors were about to go, Iktomi in his farewell said, "Come to visit us tomorrow. I invite you."

Zicha and family went out again to dine. Iktomi met them with much fine talk. "Sit upon these handsome rugs, " he said, spreading out a miserable shabby calf skin. Then to his wife he commanded, "Heat water in the kettle with red hot stones. Place it on the stake driven aslant over the center fire." He walked proudly out. Zicha and his wife looked down their noses.

Outside, they heard Iktomi trying to climb the cone shaped teepee. He went puffing and scrambling upward, tearing holes into the teepee covering, here and there. He reached the top. Pivoting dangerously there, he drew out a sharp knife and slashed himself in two. His body fell to the ground. And so there was another impish Iktomi less in the world.

The Witch Woman

The next two stories, "The Witch Woman" and "Squirrel Man and His Double," are separate versions of the same tale. The first is shaped and retold by Zitkala-Ša. The second is translated from her handwriting in Dakota. Some of the details vary, particularly toward the end of each story.

In both stories, the young woman acts heroically. She distinguishes between the good and the bad brothers, and she assists in conquering the evil forces of the witch woman. In the first rendition, Zitkala-Ša has softened some of the sexual and physical threat that is more apparent in the original language version. She has also removed some of the verbal cues that indicate the oral nature of the story.

In a village of the Dakotas there lived a very beautiful girl who was daughter of the head chief. Many young men brought valuable presents to her father, desiring to marry the maiden. Their offers were refused because no one came who was of sufficient importance to meet the chief's demand. One morning the girl's brother discovered her crying and knew the cause. He scolded her.

"You indeed wish to marry a man whose parents are poor," he said, "a good for nothing who is not even a hunter."

This angered the girl so that in the night she stole silently out of her father's tepee and fled. All the people turned out and hunted for her during two suns. At last they found her hidden among some willows. When the finders took her home, her mother spanked her soundly.

They called her Hides-in-Willows, which became her name. For a number of suns the girl's relatives watched her closely, then she again fled in the night. She did not hide but

71

ran swiftly as far as she could run. She traveled for two suns, and became very much exhausted. She was about to perish, not being able to find food. She would have fallen but saw a tepee standing against some pine trees. This gave her strength to go on a little way.

When she had come to this teepee, a young man sat in the doorway making arrows. Hides-in-Willows saw that this young man was living alone. She was perishing from hunger. A bear came out of the tepee, but she was not frightened, for the young man seemed a very proper person and the bear was his companion.

When she had waited, drooping from weariness, for a little time, the owner of the tepee looked at her kindly.

"How," he said. "What do you wish?"

"I would dwell with you," said the maiden. "I perish from hunger. Let me be your wife and keep the tepee."

"But I do not wish for a wife," said the young man earnestly. "I do not indeed wish to marry."

"Then let me be your younger sister, and call you tibdo," urged the starving girl.

"Very good," said the young man, "it shall be so."

Hides-in-Willows then became the man's younger sister and he her tibdo (elder brother). The brother was an excellent hunter and provided well for the tepee. A bear lived with them. This bear was the young man's pet, and carried his packs.

After they had thus lived for five moons, the young man said, "Younger sister, I wish to go on a journey. I shall be gone many suns. Lo, there is much papa and wasna in the bags. Therefore you will have enough of meat. Beware of Iktomi, who will come to fool you in some ways. Remember the red earring which I wear in my left ear. This you must do because I have a twin brother who resembles me closely."

Taking the bear with him, the young man went away. Some days after he had gone, Iktomi came to her tepee thinking to fool the maiden. He was dressed in smoky skins, and appeared to be a fine young man. With very pleasant manners, standing without her door, he spoke to Hides-in-Willows.

"I am come to see my brother," he said. "I did not know that he was married." But the maiden was not deceived. She shut the door in Iktomi's face. After a time another man came. This one looked so much like her brother that she would have been deceived had he worn a red earring. This man acted very badly and abused her because she could not tell where his brother was.

When he went away he said, "I will come back in four days, and you had better see that my brother is found."

On the next day the girl's real adopted brother returned and she told him all that had happened.

"The last was my twin brother," said the young man, "and he is a bad fellow. I will fight him when he returns, and if there shall be any cause for you to interfere, remember that I wear the red earring."

When the wicked brother returned, however, he was dressed exactly like the other and also wore a red earring. The two quickly quarreled and, being evenly matched, they fought until both fell upon the ground from exhaustion.

The girl came out of her tepee armed with a war club, "Which shall I kill?" she asked.

"Kill this one, sister," said one.

"Kill this one, sister," said the other.

"Well," said the girl, "I will strike the one who does not speak like my brother." Instantly, she killed the wicked one who had spoken last. Thus was the brother saved alive. They buried the body of the other under a heap of wood and burned it. While the heap was burning the flames hissed and crackled and there were sounds as of hail falling upon dry leaves. Suddenly they saw that many fine ornaments, pearls, shells, bracelets and necklaces, were thrown out of this fire which burned with a brilliant light.

"See, sister, you must not touch any of those things," said the brother. "It is wakan."

The girl stood looking at the pretty things after her brother had gone into his tepee. Presently she discovered a very fine pair of earrings, which she coveted. She glanced furtively about, then seized the pretty ornaments and hid them under her belt.

When she went into the tepee she was taken with violent pains and fell upon the ground. The brother looked at her steadily for a moment then he spoke to the bear, "See, Grandfather," he said, "the sister is very ill. Try and cure her." The bear went to the girl and walked three times around her, licking her belt. The earrings were thus dislodged and the maiden recovered.

"Younger sister," said the brother, "we shall have to go to my mother lest she come and discover what has happened. She lives to the South." They left their tepee and traveled for two suns to the Southward, going to the lodge of a witch woman who was the young man's mother. When they were near to this old woman's tepee and traveling in a wood, they came suddenly upon Iya, the eater. This huge giant, whose body is so stuffed with eating that his spindle legs can scarcely carry him about, was standing beneath a tree.

"Inhan! Inhan!" cried Iya when he saw them.[1] "So you are come fetching another wife. This one makes twenty-six. You ought to marry the earth."

"Younger sister," said the brother secretly, "you must let my mother suppose that you are my wife. She will thus believe I am her son who is dead."

Presently these two came to the lodge of the witch woman, which was surrounded by the tepees of her son's wives. The old woman's lodge was very large, and the poles inside were hung with charms and medicine bags and with many different kinds of claws and rattles. The witch woman sat in the center, and a blanket woven of human hair was hung above her head.

The son sat down by his mother. "Mother I have returned fetching a wife as you see," he said. The old woman looked far away out of the tepee door and said nothing.

That night they were awakened by noises of people shouting and singing and of drums, pum pum pum. These were people in the belly of Iya, the eater, who guarded the old witch woman's tepee.

After two or three days, the old woman began to suspect that her son who had returned was not the one who had gone away. One morning, she said, "My son, go to the woods and kill some young pigeons for your wives. Iya shall show you the way."

So the young man went with Iya, walking slowly. They found many wild pigeons. The hunter shot one, breaking its neck. Iya picked up this bird and examined it. "Your brother could not shoot in this manner," he said.

Again, a bird fell with a broken neck. Iya said, "You indeed shoot very well, and I know you now. You must not shoot birds in the neck, but in the body, else your mother will know instantly."

"Let us throw these birds away then," counseled the hunter.

"Not so," said Iya, "for then the witch woman will surely find them. Put these in the bottom of your bag and then kill a great number, four for each of the wives."

When the hunters had filled their bag with pigeons, they returned to the mother's tepee. The witch woman was well pleased. She put a great many pigeons in a rawhide kettle, and put them boiling with hot stones. There were still pigeons left in the bag, which Iya had thought to have for his share. The old woman took all the pigeons out and discovered the two with broken necks.

"Ye-e-e! Micinksin t'o tka! Alas, my son is dead!" She took a lance and her blanket and ran out to the north.

Iya said, "Let us all now fly!" All the wives seized upon such things as they could carry and ran southward over a hill. Iya had the pot of pigeons and, as he waddled on duck's legs, he was eating singing and laughing.

As the eater ran he turned his head presently and saw the witch woman chasing. She shouted at him to stop and fetch all her children back. Iya mocked at her. "See if you can catch us, old she-wizard!" he shouted.

The witch woman came on faster. She was near to Iya, and she poised her lance to hurl it. Iya dropped his pot, which burst on one side and instantly became a wall of rawhide across the earth.

Iya laughed and waddled on. The old woman attacked the wall with her knife. She was cutting through it. "Ah-ha, you villain!" she cried. "I will soon make a hole in your big stomach. You shall swallow no more camps of people!"

Iya took his long tobacco pouch from his belt. He smote the earth with this pouch and the earth cracked and a river ran there. The witch woman tumbled into this river.

"Hereafter," said Iya, "you and your children shall live under the water. You shall be called Unktehi." And so it happened. The river still runs a great distance. It is the Minisose, the Missouri.

Squirrel Man and His Double

As evidenced by correspondence in the Bonnin collection, Gertrude Bonnin was fluent and literate in Dakota. In this original language version of the story, Bonnin's distinctive script is much more meticulous than her hurried handwriting of letters and other documents. As translated by Gary Cavender, Shakopee Mdewakanton Sioux (Dakota), the story reveals verbal cues and stylistics, including running sentences and timelessness. The tale socializes hearers to the incest taboo, and possibly this topic is the reason Zitkala-Ša did not translate it but shaped it. Cavender's more literal translation provides a fascinating comparison and accentuates her role as storyteller.

Cavender commented on his rendition from the manuscript: "We can't translate word for word because there are some expressions in Dakota that just don't translate into English. English is kind of a linear language. Dakota is kind of an idea type language where you translate the idea of what you're going to say rather than [what] you would in English. The story sounds like what my grandmother used to tell me when I was a baby."[1]

A young man lives with his younger sister. His younger sister he lived with alone and the young man, her older brother, was an expert hunter. The animals roamed free. The buffalo and deer he really hunted for with his bow and arrow. He was an expert shot and killed many deer and buffalo and they lived very well and had an abundance of meat and were not in need, and so lived happy and content.

And here after the young man, her brother, went hunting, a young man came while the young lady was home alone and

Zitkala-Ša's transcription in Dakota of "Squirrel Man and His Double." Gertrude and Raymond Bonnin Collection [MSS 1704]. Courtesy of L. Tom Perry Special Collections, Harold B. Lee Library, Brigham Young University, Provo, Utah.

made advances to her and halfway through he attacked her and was trying to make her lie down with him; she cried and resisted, they say. And here the young man had the very same yellow hair as her elder brother and was very good looking as he was dressed like him with even the eagle feather he put in his hair. So she thought he was her older brother. The way her older brother dressed, his facial features and his body structure was identical to her older brother. She thought, "My brother did a very terrible thing."

The young man was bothering her again, but she refused his advances and he couldn't force her so he quit and went away. Just at the same time, her older brother came in packing a deer on his back and he was happy talking on, but the young girl (his younger sister) was very sad and quiet. "Why is my younger sister so sad?" he thought. But he did not ask her or say anything. Again he (the young man) took his bow and arrow and went to shoot deer.

But just as he left, the same young man who looked like her older brother came in and made advances and attacked her, but she protected herself crying. "My older brother doesn't do disrespectful things to me," she cried. And so he didn't succeed. This was the second time he tried this and the young girl was very heart broken. Again the young man went out somewhere and at the same time again, her older brother came back packing a deer and was happily talking to his younger sister who was very quiet again. He thought, "Why is my younger sister so quiet?" but he did not ask her.

The third time he went hunting, again the one who looked like her older brother turned and came back in. He made advances to her and halfway through, he attacked her again. She cried and said, "Older brother, have compassion for me and don't do disrespectful things to me!" (She said crying.)

"If this is my older brother, I will find out," she thought, and so the Eagle Feather that he wore in his hair, he wore the tip of it with a piece she parted that she had made a mark. The young girl was strong and when the young man attacked her he couldn't take her, so finally again he gave up and left. At the same time her older brother returned with a deer on his back and he was happily making conversation. And then her older brother, the feather he wore in his hair, she looked at it and here it was parted at the tip. She saw this and was saddened even more and thought, "For sure now it is my older brother who has been trying to attack me, this is he" (she thought). At the same time the young man who wore the feather in his hair took it and here at the tip, a part of it was stripped. He examined it and said, "I came back through some underbrush and it got caught and stripped" (he said).

He took a sealer they call glue and repaired it. And now even more she was saddened and did not look at her older brother. The young man (the older brother) thought, "Why is my younger sister so sad? She doesn't even want to look at me now. I think I'll ask her" (he thought). And so he asked her: "Younger sister, why are you so sad?" (he said). And she said, "Because, older brother, you have treated me very disrespect-fully and have made me very sad and ashamed" (she said).

And he said, "What have I done to you?" (he said). And she said, "You said you were going to marry me and then you attacked me and for your actions I am very sad and ashamed" (she said). "You have done this three times." When the young man heard he was very sad and said, "Oh! Oh! Younger sister, that is not me" (he said). And then he said, "All right, younger sister, I will stand outside here and hide. Hold on to him very tight! And attack him and I will confront him and I will fall on top of him. And I will say 'Younger sister! It is I who is on top! Hurry!' I will say. And then I will fall underneath and I will say 'Younger sister! I have fallen underneath. Hurry!' I will say" (he said). This is how he instructed his young sister. "Which ever way it happens I will be the first to say this."

It was night fall and into day break when he stood hidden somewhere. And the young man who came there was there again and went inside. The young man had very long hair. So the young girl grabbed a hold of his hair very hard and said,

"Older brother! Come on!" She was yelling and her older brother came running and came inside. She still had a hold of him so both of the men attacked each other, and here the two of them were identical and had yellow hair, and were very tall and of the same build. And so it was difficult to tell which one was her elder brother. They bounced around inside the dwelling and fell down on top of each other. And here the one on top said, "Younger sister! The one on top is me! Just as I said." And then the one that was lying underneath said, "Young sister! The one lying underneath is me just as I told you" (he said).

And so the young girl had an ax and was chasing them with it, but she couldn't make out which one was her older brother.

"Well even so," she thought, "which ever one is first to say 'this is me' it will be my older brother, as he did say he would be the first to say that. And so the one underneath is not the one perhaps," she thought, and the one underneath, with the ax, she crushed and killed him, and he died.

And the young man said, "Younger sister, in the center of the dwelling we will dig deep into the ground and bury him" (he said). And the young girl said "Yes" and dug deep in the ground in the center of the dwelling and buried him. They did this and built a fire outside because the dwelling was just a common tent and therefore the fire in the center of the dwelling would not be visible.

And here there was these two young men who fought. These two, they were called squirrel and that was what they were. And therefore, for sure, they were so much alike, they were like one.

And here the young man said to his younger sister, "Some helpers are coming, but they are all bad. And so I will say I married you and the young man we killed, they will think was me" (he said). "Don't be shamed, this way they won't kill us," he said.

And so a bear and a black bear, and a panther and a giant,

these four came. Where the young man and his sister sat very close to each other they came and stood. And then the young man said to the four that came, "Ho, my sons have come. Son, this is your mother" (he said). "Cook for my sons and they shall eat," he told his younger sister. A very large kettle, the largest one she used to cook for them. Four deer she cooked for them. When it was cooked, the four beings, they gave to them and they ate it all up. And of the four that came, the bear quietly sat in attention and whispered, "For sure this is not father," he said to the others and stood up and left. And then sometime later again, the black bear said, whispering to the others, "This is not father," and stood up and left. And later again, the panther said, "This is not father" (he said). He stood up and left and the giant alone sat there and said, "Older brother, last evening the young man you killed, his mother will be coming" (he said). "So soon as we can head back that way," he said, "I will say that young man you killed was you. I will say, and what you need to do so they won't kill you, I will teach you," the giant said.

And so the three of them, the giant, the young man and the young girl were going back and here they came upon a red dressed hidden tipi standing they came upon and stood by. And the giant said, "Older brother, sit down here and comb your sister's hair" (he said). And so he combed his younger sister's hair. "And then, I will go first," the giant said, and he went and ventured there. And he said, "Mother, older brother married and they have returned and settled here, and he is combing his wife's hair" (he said). The giant told his mother about the young man they killed and the woman looked over and said, "My son lives, he is not dead and he is married" (she said). And then the young man and his younger sister stood up, went to the red tipi, and stood outside. And the giant stood before them and whispered, "Older brother, when you enter, go to your west" (he said). "They have rules," he said. The tipi door faced south and so he went inside and went toward the west and went around the fire and south toward the door they went and sat down. And the head woman said, "Truly this is my son" (she said). And here inside there were nine young girls with very beautiful faces and here the young man they killed was married to all of them. And here the young man went outside and the giant went to him and told him, "Older brother, tomorrow the head woman will tell you to shoot some doves" (he said). "And she will tell you to take a large bag with you," he said, "and that you will fill to the fullest and if you don't fill the bag full, she will know you are not her child. For that reason she will do this" (he said). "When her child that was killed would go shooting doves, he filled a bag full of doves he shot" (he said). "And then you do not take your bow and arrow, she will tell you to take a very small bow and arrow" (he said). "And also she will tell you to shoot the doves right in the center of their heads," the giant said. "And if she sees that you have shot some of them in their bodies, she will know that you are not her child." These things the giant said.

It was past night time now and it was day break and here she told the young man to take the small bow and arrow. So he took them and then she gave him a huge sack. And the giant went with him and now he was shooting the doves right in the center of their head. And the sack was very full and they headed for home and arrived. And the head woman took the doves one by one and examined their heads. Again, she would take another and examine it. Finally, she examined all of them and of them shot right in the center of their heads. And then she said, "Surely this is my son" (she said). "But then again, some things have me thinking otherwise," she added.

Now the night has passed and it is day break. The head woman wrapped herself in a leather robe and a stone club she had. She took it and went to the place where her son was killed and buried. And the giant said, "Older brother! We must flee! Her child you killed she went to look for and surely she will know when she gets there, we must flee now!" (the giant said). And the young man said, "We will do that" (he said). And then the giant took the woman's bag and dumped the contents and he took a bundle of curdled dry blood and also an oak tree root as large as a human finger nail. He took with these in hand and they fled, ten young girls, and the giant and the young man made twelve. Together they ran and they had gone a long way. They looked and here in two directions white smoke appeared upwards. The tipi where the young man and his younger sister lived, she set on fire and she showed how angry she was. And then where she lived, white smoke was coming. Again she returned there but they had fled. She was so angry she set everything on fire in her anger. She did this, they thought, so with all their might they ran. They sweat so much, they sat down to cool off.

In that instant the woman appeared near by and they stood up and with all their might they fled. But the woman was faster and closing in. The giant was very slow and she was catching up to him close. The woman said, "You hateful giant, wherever you go, I will kill you! And your hair is bad but with it I will trim the bottom of my robe" (she said). She ran after him with her stone club aimed at him. But the giant was not even afraid, and laughed and laughed with his big belly he ran.

And the giant said, "Older brother, whatever happens, she will kill me now" (he said). But the young man said, "You yourself, my little brother, do something!" "All right," he said. And he dumped the dry curdled blood. He threw it away and the ground on one side turned muddy and sticky and curdled and it was impassable.

So the woman was unable to cross. She walked along the side but she couldn't get through. And here on the side of the bank, two cranes with long, long necks stood. And the woman said, "Crane, I want to get to the other side but I'm unable to" (she said). "So if you put your necks together, I can walk across on them," she said.

The other crane said, "If we do this and you get on this side what are you going to compensate us with?" (he said).

"I promise one of you will marry me," she said.

"All right, that is fine what you said," they said. Then both of them lay down on the bank with their heads together and so their necks reached across. And she walked over them and reached the other bank and here she said to the cranes: "Oh! You stand here as if to marry, you worthless. I should marry one or the other," she said to them and ran with all her might.

They had gone a long ways, but truly this woman was very swift they say. And so she again was catching up to them. She came closer, but the giant was so slow she had her stone club aimed at him. And the woman said, "You good for nothing big belly! Your hair is ugly, but I will use it to trim my robe" (she said).

But the giant laughed, running, and said, crying, "What shall I do?" And he himself said, "My younger brother, you, what would you do?" (he said). And the giant took the oak tree root the size of a finger nail and threw it backwards. And where it fell, a huge oak tree grew upward. It lay so nothing could get through. And the woman who was a traditional Dakota could make a fire out of something she had. With that she made a fire in the center of the tree. She went through this and chased them and when she caught up to them she had her stone club in hand after the giant to kill him.

And the giant said, "Older brother, do something. She is going to kill me now!"

But the young man said, "My younger brother, you do something!"

And the giant said, "All right." And he stomped the ground very hard and the earth split very deep. And the woman fell in and the earth came back together. And the woman never came out again, they say, cousin! That is the end. Cousin, I will tell one again but it is just a common story, they say. The first people story is what it is they say, cousin. It is not a folk tale but is an oral tradition, they say.

Child Dancer, Pi-Yeh-Kah-Nump— Transfigured

Under treaty agreements, tribal members received rations to com-
pensate for lost lands and to accommodate the disappearance of
the buffalo as a major food source. Although the time is not fixed
in this story, it must be after 1870, since after that date "a head of
household drew for every family member a portion of beef, flour,
sugar, salt, coffee, tobacco, soap, clothing and more" (Hoover 36).
Zitkala-Ša consistently and vehemently wrote against tribal and
individual dependence on the federal government.

This story begins like other mythic retellings. Instead of turn-
ing to a supernatural conflict between good and evil, however, the
details seem more intended to idealize material culture elements
of the past. The caring behavior of the family members toward one
another contrasts the individual isolation and desperation of the
later scenes.

Beside the brightly burning camp fire, Pi-Yeh-Kah-Nump [Lit-
tle Sugar] danced with tiny moccasined feet. Her father, sitting
on the ground with crossed shins, sang and beat the drum
lightly. Summer evenings are memorable for these happy
reunions of the family after a busy day of hunting deer. The
mother broiled venison on the red embers. The evening meal
over, Little Sugar's mother piled dry sticks on the fire, coaxing
the flames into joyous blazes. She laughed with contentment,
watching her baby girl bouncing with so much vim.

The father spoke to some one. "How. Come into our circle
of light. Be seated." He pointed to a grass mat. A toothless
grandmother of the tribe stood on the outer edge of the light,
resting her wrinkled chin on her long willow cane, hands
clasped over it. She too was looking at the child dancer. The
song and drum awakened memories long slumbering in her
heart.

Sugar ceased her dancing, cuddled into her father's arms, and shyly eyed the old grandmother.

"Grandchild! My tribal grandchild!" the old woman began, in a tremulous voice. "I come to sing your name, sweet child. I am poor and ragged. I need new garments. I ask for help singing your name!" This was an ancient custom of the Indian tribe. In a thin high voice, the tribal grandmother sang an old, old tune, inserting and reiterating the name, "Pi-Yeh-Kah-Nump," "Sweeter than Sugar." She finished her song with the usual mystic bird call trilled on the tip of the tongue.

Proudly Sugar's mother opened a parfleche pouch and deftly adorned the tribal grandmother in fringed deerskins. She smoothed the frowzy white locks and covered the countless wrinkles on either high cheek with warm red paint. The old grandmother again raised her voice in song. This time it was a song of praise and gratitude. The village people, attracted by the ceremonial songs, came quietly hither. They were silent witnesses in the outside darkness. They joined their voices with the grandmother's, and burst into a loud chorus, spontaneous, irresistible. The song ended, the tribal grandmother shook hands with Pi-Yeh-Kah-Nump—"Sweeter than Sugar"—and her parents. She went away rejoicing. The crowd dispersed, homeward bound to their teepees. All sounds of laughter, song, and monotones subsided into stillness of the night. With pleasant dreams Sleep over took and beguiled them, each and all.

Silently active, one hundred years have scrolled their frosty vibrations upon chubby-Indian-girl, Sugar, dancing fairy like before a cheery camp fire.

The fire is gone. The dead ashes have mingled and lost themselves in the deep soil. The very place would have been lost to the memory of men but for sensitive, Seer Indians, men and women, who from time to time chanced to camp there. They tell strange stories of the reappearance of those long departed who query after Pi-Yeh-Kah-Nump. They had left her far behind on the earth trail.

Poor little Sugar, petted and spoiled by over fond parents,

sung to in tribal ceremonies, found life harsh and very stern. She rebelled that she could not have all her whims satisfied. She grew more and more stubborn. She mourned the death of all her family and near relatives. Their going away left her solitary. The long years thereafter, which brought such inflow of noisy children, helpless as they were thoughtless, became intolerable to her. She lived alone with her pet dogs. Old Sugar has become a recluse, well nigh forgot by the younger generations.

Stranger than any dream is the amazing fact Sugar is now a centenarian herself!

White haired, toothless, wrinkled, and bent over, "Sweeter than Sugar" is beyond recognition. She is dressed in rags and tatters, but there is no place of appeal. The ancient custom of singing the name of a beloved child and asking help from more fortunate ones was long ago forgotten. Neither could she overcome her family pride enough to sing songs praying for aid. It is unthinkable. She lives on the sage hens, grouses, and rabbits the hounds bring home to her. There are many lean days, but this is preferable. Her name is still on the Tribal Ration Roll. Each month she draws her scanty portion in bitterness of spirit.

With a faded blanket fastened loosely about her, Old Sugar rides her pinto pony across the sage country, her seven wolfhounds following behind. It is another Ration Day and she is going to the Agency to receive her dole.

Most of the people of the tribe are gathering at the Agency for the same purpose.

Old Sugar arrives in front of the Issue House, dismounts, and drops the bridle reins to the ground. This the pony understands to mean "Stand here till my return." The pony obeys. The wolf hounds lay round about awaiting the return of their mistress.

Hobbling slowly, carrying a long cane, Old Sugar reaches the crowded entrance way. There is a secret nudging of elbows of those who glimpse her from the corner of their eyes. No one offers help to the Tribal Grandmother. No one speaks a word of greeting.

Old Sugar talks tauntingly to her estranged kinsmen: "You

remind me of a corral of balky herds! You mill around in circles for a dole that neither fills nor enriches you. Could our noble ancestors see you today, they would mourn, cut their hair short and cry aloud as for the dead!" Thereupon she draws from her belt a long sharp knife, swings the keen blade from side to side in front of herself. Does she intend to mow them down? She strikes at no particular one, but the crowd divides in twain before the swinging knife. A pathway is instantly cleared and open. Old Sugar shuffles forward still swinging the knife.

Momentarily the people are awed by the words of their Tribal Grandmother, but few can fathom their meaning. They watch her receive the small ration, totally inadequate. Straightway she hobbles out of the Issue House, hurrying back to her pony and the wolf hounds watching for her return.

The hungry dogs sniff at the bag of meat and bones. A quick rebuke from Old Sugar settles them. "Get down!" she says in her own tongue, for Sugar does not speak English, and the seven hounds lie down in a semicircle, their fore feet and long noses pointing toward her but their shiny eyes upon the meat bag.

Talking continuously to them, Old Sugar throws them tidbits of meat trimmed from her ration with her huge knife, calling each dog by name and to which each one responds. Toothless Old Sugar munches on a piece of hard bread. She smokes laurel leaves in a long stemmed pipe.

The sun is far past the zenith. It takes so long doing next to nothing.

The repast finished, Old Sugar prepares to go home. She ties her ration bag next to her ragged bedding roll. As if dissatisfied with the small size of her pack, she picks up four five-gallon oil cans, empties that were thrown away behind the Trading Store. These she ties on to make a great showing. Patiently but with much awkwardness, Old Sugar tries to mount her pony from a large rock. There is long delay. No longer agile, Old Sugar cannot leap into the saddle but is compelled to climb laboriously into it. A precarious undertaking for one a hundred years old. Nothing daunted, Old Sugar whacks the pony's flank with her cane. The pony is not close enough to the rock. The pony understands and, instead of jumping away from the whip, moves carefully, closer to the rock upon which Old Sugar stands ready to mount.

At last she is safely seated in the native made saddle, high pommels front and back, to which are tied tin cans and many bundles—a sight which made the Agency folk gasp. Hands were held tightly over mouths so that no sound of exclamation could escape.

Pi-Yeh-Kah-Nump, the once "Sweeter than Sugar," waves no fond farewells. Looking neither right nor left, she rides ——— disdainfully away from the Agency and its idle mob of hangers-on so much detested by her. The seven lanky wolf hounds trail behind toward the setting sun. Day wanes into twilight. Old Sugar and her wolf hounds disappear into the heart of the sage-purple plains.

Old Sugar is gone, unsung and unadorned.

Search for Bear Claws, the Lost School Boy

In this narrative, Zitkala-Ša returns to the preeminent themes from her early autobiographical writings. She privileges the tribal knowledge and traditions that will lead to the discovery of the lost boy and criticizes the influence and impact of forced education that prompted him to run away. Like "The Soft-Hearted Sioux" (American Indian Stories 109–25), the story's conclusion plays on sentiment to encourage social outrage.

In a log Dance House, Indian people sat on the floor, against the walls. The center pole was decorated gaily with bright colored paints and a long festoon of eagle feathers. Near the center pole, surrounding the drummers, sat the singers. This was a secret meeting.

A gaunt figure stood before them. His black eyes burning and flashing in their sunken sockets as he spoke: "My kinsmen, you have been kind, riding your ponies over our many hills in search for my lost boy. He is only nine summers and lonesome for our teepee. I placed him in a government boarding school, to learn the White man's language, to become a useful interpreter to our tribe, but the child is unhappy taken afar, and is ever running away from school. In this cold midwinter, my small son has fled the school again. He was lost in the blizzard three days ago."

Interrupted by moaning cries of the boy's mother, who sat with her head covered with a blanket, he paused till the pitiful wails were smothered within the folds of her robe. He continued, "We have searched the hills and the low lands in vain. All tracks have been covered with deep snow. In my despair, I returned often to the boarding school where my son was last seen. I asked the schoolman, 'Where is my son? I left him in your care. What have you done with him?' The schoolman is vexed by my repeated calls and shouted angrily, 'He ran away! He deserves a sound thrashing!' I am not hard of hearing but this schoolman yells at me; he lifts his iron eyes upward, shakes his bald head, and begins rubbing the palms of his hands together, as if to rub away some unseen bloodstains. My teeth are set in bitterness at his queer behavior and brutish lack of sympathy. The schoolman cares only for books and papers. I love my little son so much that in my desperation I defy man-made law, the missionaries and government policemen forbidding our mystics from practise of our ancient wisdom.

"Tonight I have invited our tribal Seer to help us in the search for my son. You are invited here to witness what takes place. I am eager to get some word about my boy."

Voices from all parts of the Dance House assented sympathetically, "How!" "How!" "Han!" "Be it so!" "We will be cautious!"

The bereaved father spoke no more. He sat down on the floor where he had been standing.

The musicians began humming softly a sacred chant known to the tribe but which they had not dared to sing fearing lest they be cast into prison by their petty overlords. The drummers muffled their drum beats.

The Seer, a man of medium height and strongly muscled, stepped toward the center pole. His moccasined feet were noiseless. He moved about lightly in spite of his robust figure. His long black braids fell forward over each ear. With slender fingers he touched his tambourine, and the many small bells on it tinkled like falling drops of water.

The anxiously waiting people, sitting on their feet around the walls of the Dance House, were not at all afraid. They understood the ceremonies of the tribal Seer. Their part was to keep silent, a difficult task for untrained, boisterous folk, but for them an easy thing.

The Seer spoke in a firm, positive voice: "Let the keepers of the fire put out the light." Immediately the flames were reduced by pulling apart the burning sticks and cooling the flames in the ashes. The room was dark. The Seer began singing and thrumming his small tambourine. He rattled also the clustered deer hoofs he used on such occasions.

Presently, while the Seer still sang his mystery song, the clustered deer hoofs seemed to fly out of his hand, first here and then there—sometimes it sounded from the ceiling.

The song ceased. The Seer again spoke, as if addressing someone unseen by the others within the Dance House, though they peered from their corners toward the Center Pole, where the Seer was performing his magic.

"Yes, you go at once. Find the trail of the lost school boy, Bear Claws. His parents desire to know where he is, what has happened to him. Bring me word promptly."

There was no audible response.

For many heart beats, the Seer sat motionless while his clustered deer hoofs flew about the Dance House, rattling, rattling.

Now addressing some invisible helper, the Seer said, "You have done well. We are grateful to you for this service." The Seer addressed the people: "Listen—for I have word for you about the missing boy. Follow the instructions and you will find him." The people sat breathless. "It is now midnight—tomorrow is nearly here. At sun rise, go on ponyback to the Twin Hills. Wait at the top of the West Hill and on the East you will see a lonely prairie wolf sitting on his haunches on the hill side. The wolf will turn his nose to the sky and howl so fast, it will sound like cries from a pack of them. He will trot away. In line with the wolf and where you stand look carefully down the ravine between the Twin Hills; there will be seen a small cloth blown by the North wind. When you see this, go there. That bit of cloth sticking up through the crusted snow is the corner of the pocket flap on the coat worn by the run-away school boy."

With muttered exclamations, the crowd went noiselessly away to their dwellings. Only the father and his scouts lingered to plan their ride to the Twin Hills.

Before day break, the grief-stricken father and his friends were mounted on their surefooted ponies and riding slowly toward the Twin Hills. Dawn revealed the searching party silhouetted against an empty sky, waiting on the hilltop, shivering with cold and with anguish, their eyes turned eastward for the light.

At length the sun rose over the horizon. Lo! they beheld the lonely prairie wolf on the hillside, resting upon its haunches, pointing his sharp nose to the gray sky and howling furiously. Then he trotted on his way out of sight.

The Indian men on their ponies remained like statues. They scanned the white snow on hillside and deep ravine. A tiny black speck appeared in the wide stretches of snow. It was in the bottom of the ravine. In silence broken only by the crunching pony hoofs in crusted snow, the sorrowful father of little Bear Claws led his party down the hill. They dismounted beside the bit of dark cloth protruding through the deep snow. There under the snow blanket they found the run-away school boy's body. Little Bear Claws was gone away where boarding schools can no more torture.

Prayer of Pe-Šnija— Shriveled-Top

The verisimilitude of this story marks Zitkala-Ša's shift toward a more realistic style of writing that details the circumstances and trials of reservation life. She pits traditional experience against the demands of institutional Christianity, like in "Why I Am a Pagan" and "The Soft-Hearted Sioux" (American Indian Stories 101–25). When these pieces are considered outside the context of her whole life it becomes easy to assume that Bonnin privileges traditional beliefs to the exclusion of Christianity. The greater challenge is to try and understand how she could be so critical yet remain faithful.

Pe-Šnija means "sparks of fire," but Snija means "withered."

Unfortunately, the last part of the manuscript is missing and Pe-Šnija's prayer remains unknown.

Along the river bottom, cone shaped teepees were clustered adjacent to an abandoned military post. Plains Indians lived together in family group formation.[1] Daily men and women walked to the Trading Store at the Post now converted into an Indian Agency where the government stationed its employees and missionaries.

By twos and threes, as the Plains people trudged to the Agency, they expressed their views secretly to one another. One man observed, "The Government's flag is always up over the Missionary's house." The vacated ware-house had been assigned to the Missionary, and he had established his church there. The couple walked on apace in silence, then the other old warrior looked afar off, with a hand shading his eyes, as if to sight some moving armies, then he looked up at the bright sun over-head, and, turning to his companion, he said; "As the

Sun hears me, I vow that flag queers the long sermons preached to us by the Missionary. The Government Agent told our tribe they must attend the church meetings, that they must listen to the sermons, if they dared to disobey, they would have to answer to the flag. The Agent pointed a claw like finger at that flag, and I understood his full meaning. Soldiers would be sent to kill us and our children."

Mothers with bright eyed babes on their backs followed in the well trodden foot path. Shouting boys and girls played beside them, running about with their sliding willow sticks. The laughter of children drowned the low, somber words of the men as they passed by them. This was the day of doles at the Agency. All were going hither to draw their portion of the rations. In lieu of former self-subsistence by hunting, the government had made treaties with the Dakota promising them that as long as they could not support themselves within the reservation in which they were corralled, so long would rations be issued them. There were murmurs of dissatisfaction among the people as they drew their small issues of beef, green coffee and sugar, a few scoops of flour, and small baking powder. These rations hardly compensated for the loss of freedom, the joy of the hunt, and abundance of wild game they once had.

Crowds loitered in the Trading Store. Indians brought red stone pipes and beaded bags to trade for crackers, matches, and candy. Pe-Šnija was a regular customer. He was a professional wood chopper for government employees. For his labors, much or little, he accepted only the thin silver coin and rejected all other coins for pay. He had money to spend occasionally. Those who had no money to spend stood chattering in a light vein to cover up their embarrassment. Pe-Šnija, bronzed by summer suns, with long jet braids over each ear and a perfectly smooth face, joined with the loafers in their hearty laughter. The funniest jokes were about the beard and mustache on the Paleface.

[*Second page of manuscript is missing.*]

Dreams

By the time Zitkala-Ša wrote this piece, she had reentered the world of publishing and had been editing American Indian Magazine. *She had turned from fiction and storytelling to expository writing. She explains the circumstances of her life and demonstrates her compelling interest in social and political issues. The emphasis on the Sioux leaders may have been prelude to the Sioux factionalism within the Society of American Indians.*

I.

On the night of June 11, 1919, I had a very interesting dream preceded by a tiny, laughable one of four elder Indian men. Two were Sioux, and of the old school type. I walked with them, engaged in conversation about the Society of American Indians work. The other two men were of a different tribe, and stood aloof. One of the Sioux men stepped aside to talk with one of them about our organization, with a view to gaining the two as members. Silently the fourth man stood, listening to the words of the Sioux addressing his comrade. The other Sioux, with whom I waited, called to his Sioux friend, "Do not take so much time to talk to him now. Tell him anything that will quickly induce him to join us!" This is the Sioux language, thinking that the other men could not understand. Then the Sioux who was doing the coaxing answered back, "That is just the way to do it, but every time I say anything to him he answers me in Sioux!" (End of tiny dream.)

I woke up in the night, and, remembering the embarrassed expressions on the faces of the two elderly and very dignified Sioux men, I laughed aloud!

2.

Again, I no sooner went to sleep when I fell into another dream. This time it was a long dream and peopled with three white women and a cute little white child, my husband, and myself. Mention was made of Old Sioux,[1] an old Indian whom I had taken care of for some twelve years, though not a blood relative, who had passed into the beyond three years ago.

I found myself in a spacious hall, looking on during the rendition of a program. Whatever this entertainment was, the three ladies, who appeared to be very chummy, were directly responsible. One, being the chief artist, directed it throughout the evening. While I failed to catch the thread of the story, life-like pictures protruded from the high walls, first in one place, then again in another place, picture succeeding picture. I felt a vague sense of many pictures appearing and disappearing all around me so noiselessly and rapidly that I could not look upon any one of them as much as I wished.

At last my attention became riveted upon a picture of a barn loft, where through the loose hay were hidden hundreds of white eggs. I was dumbfounded to learn through the inaudible atmosphere of the hall that Old Sioux, whom I had befriended when so poor upon earth, had been hiding these eggs. I felt a bit hurt that he had not been moved to share them with us while he lived in my home. A small girl with a fluffy dress, who had been attracted by the sight of the eggs, tiptoed easily up the wall to the edge of the picture, and there stood looking at them. While this picture seemed to be linked with my life somehow, perhaps because Old Sioux was in the story, it had no special interest to the Chief Lady Artist who was responsible for the realistic and yet artistic metaphysical illustrations. Neither could I see how they came on, nor what governed their order.

I saw the Lady Artist standing at her place but did not watch her closely, as the pictures appearing and disappearing were very fascinating to me. There on another wall from where the barn loft had been portrayed, appeared a great crystal window through which I looked out upon a wide lake. On its flat, sandy beach I beheld about six white camels following in a trail, one after the other headed toward me. I know they were conjured up for the occasions yet so life-like were they that I could not help exclaiming, "How do you accomplish these real and yet unreal pictures?" I turned a moment to the Lady Artist as I spoke. Instantly the placid lake, sandy beach, white camels, and window vanished! I wondered just how the physical seeming and spiritual reality were interwoven, and how these three women had mastered the secret so well that they were now using their power in this wonderful, absorbing program. There came to me a sense of having gotten a clue to this new art myself. I became exhilarated by the sense of having gained a new power. I believed I too would be able to bring forth these wonderfully realistic yet fantastic illustrations to support my own line of work. It would hasten its successful achievement. It made me rejoice!

The program ended. The three ladies put on their dark, broad-brimmed straw hats trimmed with dashing bows of red and black ribbon drawn into long loops. These loops were cut at the ends to sharp points. One of the three hats differed from the other two by a slight touch of gray ribbon added to the red and black.

Watching them preparing to leave, I seemed to have thought aloud, for I did not intend to speak about being reluctant to bring out some of my work. There was a feeling of hesitancy lest I appear to be seeking undue public credit. The Lady Artist, stopping momentarily in pinning on her hat, replied in a voice full of rebuke, "Why, don't you know that the doer cannot sever himself or herself from the deed? You cannot if you tried! You belong to the deed, you are a part of it. To withhold yourself, even for a time, is to mar the wholeness of the story or picture you have made." All this I seemed to understand and was glad it was in harmony with her masterful doctrine. Then the three ladies left.

The hall was empty.

I turned to a great post where a small mirror hung. Leaning forward, I started to tuck some loose ends of short hair into the coils pinned securely on the top of my head. I was utterly surprised to see in the glass that my hair had turned white! My husband stood waiting beside me though I had been wholly oblivious of his presence the whole time the wonderful pictures were being given. I remarked to him, "Isn't it strange that my hair should turn so white in such a short time?" to which he acquiesced.

Poems

Poetry is a genre for which Bonnin is least known and is not where she excelled. Apparently her first pieces written for publication, the two student poems from The Earlhamite, *indicate that she was more comfortable with prose narrative. Indeed, these works and her later poems in* American Indian Magazine *are more storytelling than poetic.*

The poems generally seem controlled by their rhyme and meter and have an artificially high rhetoric consistent with sentimental verse of the period. Nevertheless, the themes of Bonnin's poetry are similar to those of her other writings. These early writings reveal in a variety of genres her passion for topics and issues with which she wrestled throughout her life. She writes of struggle and resistance, nature, and romance. Bonnin's conviction for political imperative appears forcefully in "The Indian's Awakening," her first publication in American Indian Magazine. *In her poems, she incorporates the familiar, like the parody of "My Country 'Tis of Thee" in "The Red Man's America," with the tribally specific and politic.*

Ballad

"Ballad" tells a romantic story of Winona and Osseolo. "Winona," a common Sioux female name, is derived from the Dakota word for firstborn girl. Bonnin will use it again for the female lead in The Sun Dance Opera. *"Osseolo" refers to Seminole resistance leader, Osceola (ca. 1804–38). Though not written in ballad meter, the narrative structure of the poem is conventional and includes classical and Biblical allusions.*

Afar on rolling western lands
There cluster cone-like cabins white,
There roam the brave, the noble bands.
A race content with each day's light.

> Say not, "This nation has no heart
> In which strong passions may vibrate;"
> Say not, "Deep grief can play no part."
> For mute long suffering is innate.

Above the village on the plain
Dark, threatening clouds of brooding woe
Hang like some hovering monster Pain
With wicked eye on Peace, its foe.

> Once e'er Aurora[1] had proclaimed
> Approaching charioteer of Day,
> Distress, with frozen heart, controlled
> This village with unbounded sway.

What means this rushing to and fro?
Sad, anxious faces? Grieving eyes?
Now surging tears brave hearts o'erflow
In sobs that melt the sterner sighs.

Poems

What means the neighing steeds arrayed
With boughs cut fresh from living green
A dark foreboding they betrayed
In pawings fierce and sniffings keen.

> Apart from this confusion strayed
> Winona to the watering place,
> A spring with mighty rocks part stayed
> Like sacred water in rude vase.

'Tis here her nag with glossy coat,
The brisk young Wala, loves to graze.
Alert, she hears a low, clear note.
The call Winona gave always.

> Nor long was Wala innocent
> That ills now bowed Winona low.
> But see, perchance by fates well sent,
> Comes tall and proud Osseolo.

By grief made bold, Winona shy,
Half chiding, questioned her heart's king;
Yet even reproach was lost well nigh
In mingling with the murm'ring spring.

> "But stay, Osseolo," she prayed:
> Did you not hear the angry cry
> Of howling wolves that last night stayed
> Within the deep ravines near by?

"Did you not hear the moody owl
In mournful hoots foreboding ill.
With warnings of the Fate's dark scowl
That all of yesterday did fill?

> "To-day as I my Wala called,
> I roused the sullen, sacred bird,
> Which merely sight of me appalled.
> Nor ceased to shriek, in flight e'en heard.

"Osseolo, you dare not go,
Ambitious though perchance for fame.
Our gods, 'tis clear, are with the foe,
And wars without our gods bring shame."

    In deep, sad tones, like muffled bell,
    The curfew of their love on earth
    It seemed, and bitter tears did well
    Within her heart foredoomed to death.

Winona's fear was dreaded fact.
"My chieftain father," he replied,
"Did ask me as a leader act,
And I, a loyal son, complied.

    "'Tis thoughts of you shall make me strong.
    Though hard and cruel 'tis to part:
    But hark! I bear the farewell song
    Begun, the signal for our start."

Soon Wala bore Osseolo
Fast o'er receding hill and vale.
Like breathing arrow from the bow
She urged the space from village wail.

    For on that day of rounded moon
    There would be heard a festive strain
    Of hostile bands they planned at noon
    To pounce upon and glory gain.

Here too was Judas of this tribe,
A silent, plotting traitor base,
Whom jealousy and Hate did bribe
In hands of foe this plan to place.

    Osseolo, though brave and bold,
    Was not prepared to meet his foe
    Forearmed with his own plottings sold
    Together with the cruel bow.

Like jungle fight was battle din,
When elephant and tiger groan.
In bloody conflict one must win,
'Mid thundering roar and dying moan.

　　The hoarse uproar of fallen ones
　　Was pierced by pain and death-fraught cry
　　Of wounded horse. The life blood runs
　　In streams too strong to ever dry.

Winona is of friend bereaved!
A crouching, wounded form passed on
To death. But Wala's heart now sheathed
His cruel sword. The traitor's gone.

　　Osseolo unconscious lay
　　Amid the mass in deeper sleep
　　Till cooling breath of waning day
　　Aroused his senses Death would keep.

Although secure in bands of foe,
Recovered life brought with it hope
To one whose needed strength did flow
From thoughts of home with fate to cope.

　　But clings like poisoned dart, his lot.
　　In three days hence a sacrifice
　　To gods of war he would be brought,
　　A future favor to entice.

With gnawing hunger, burning throat,
And eyes that ached for want of sleep,
O'er him one day and night did float
Like lingering flights from Fiery Deep.

　　An eagle from his lofty nest,
　　With greedy eye fast on his prey.
　　Were not more sure his aim to test
　　Than that ill-fated, dreaded day.

As now it poises overhead
The narrow space of two brief nights,
The hope of all escape lies dead,
Too vivid are funereal rites.

    Defeat held every plan for flight,
    Which maddened him with wild despair.
    The torture did surpass his might.
    His cup o'erflowed with pain, its care.

The second night dispelled the light,
With it the captive's reason fled.
Or seemed to flee from frenzied might.
Osseolo seemed madness-led.

    That harsh and empty laugh is his,
    That makes your heart so numb and cold,
    Once proud—now reeling judgment's his
    That blinds your eyes with pain untold.

And Rumor soon the story spread.
Men did, with knowing faces, nod
In movement slow that plainly said,
"Our captive's doomed e'en by a god."

    The third and final day was spent
    In singing loud resounding praise
    Of all the gods appeased who sent
    The sacrifice they soon would raise.

That night, though heaven darkly frowned,
And great black clouds did veil her face
They reason in their vict'ry drowned,
Did boisterous revelry embrace.

    And even faithful guards did dare
    To join the band of braves renowned.
    And thus they threw aside all care
    Of him whom fates, they said, had bound.

But with the rushing, rising tide
Of thousand laughing voices rose
The captive's trampled, swollen pride,
And boundaries of his heart o'erflows.

    Then passed from out the prison gate
    A figure proudly straight and tall,
    Like spirit for its wand'rings late,
    It glided past the prison wall.

The evening twilight of next day
Found by the spring Winona lone
To bathe with tears the sad moon's ray,
To add heart-groans to spring's low moan.

    Was it a voice from spirit land
    That called in accents so well known
    Or was it only memory's band
    That led from worded keys the tone?

No more the moonbeams seemed to pine,
But fell like tiny, downy flakes,
Amid the heart's deep sea of brine,
And sweetened it e'en as the lakes.

    No more is heard the spring's low moan,
    It fell like spray of tinkling bells.
    Winona is no more alone,
    And now a joy all grief dispels.

New life for her begins to flow,
Her heart grows warm and eyes grow bright.
A wilted flower revived can grow!
Osseolo is back this night.

The Earlhamite 3.7 (Jan. 9, 1897): 97–98.

Iris of Life

Another student poem by Gertrude Simmons, "Iris of Life" has a lyricism that is subtly underscored by the burden of life's experiences.

Like tiny drops of crystal rain,
    in every life the moments fall,
To wear away with silent beat,
    The shell of selfishness o'er all.

And every act, not one too small,
    That leaps from out the heart's pure glow,
Like ray of gold sends forth a light,
    While moments into seasons flow.

Athwart the dome, Eternity,
    To Iris grown resplendent, fly
Bright gleams from every noble deed
    Till colors with each other vie.

'Tis glimpses of this grand rainbow,
    Where moments with good deeds unite,
That gladden many weary hearts,
    Inspiring them to seek more Light.

The Earlhamite 5 (Nov. 1, 1898): 31.

The Indian's Awakening

Fifteen years later Zitkala-Ša reiterates many of the resentments toward assimilative educational practices found in "The School Days of an Indian Girl" (American Indian Stories 47–80). The tone of desolation and separation from tribal ties is more prominent here than in other writings as she seems to seek comfort from a higher power. There remains a frank acknowledgment that even Christ had not rid the world of racism.

I snatch at my eagle plumes and long hair.
A hand cut my hair; my robes did deplete.
Left heart all unchanged; the work incomplete.
These favors unsought, I've paid since with care.
Dear teacher, you wished so much good to me,
That though I was blind, I strove hard to see.
Had you then, no courage frankly to tell
Old race-problems, Christ e'en failed to expel?

My light has grown dim, and black the abyss
That yawns at my feet. No bordering shore;
No bottom e'er found by hopes sunk before.
Despair I of good from deeds gone amiss.
My people, may God have pity on you!
The learning I hoped in you to imbue
Turns bitterly vain to meet both our needs.
No Sun for the flowers, vain planting seeds.

I've lost my long hair; my eagle plumes too.
From you my own people, I've gone astray.
A wanderer now, with no where to stay.
The Will-o-the-wisp learning, it brought me rue.

It brings no admittance. Where I have knocked
Some evil imps, hearts, have bolted and locked.
Alone with the night and fearful Abyss
I stand isolated, life gone amiss.

Intensified hush chills all my proud soul.
Oh, what am I? Whither bound thus and why?
Is there not a God on whom to rely?
A part of His Plan, the atoms enroll?
In answer, there comes a sweet Voice and clear,
My loneliness soothes with sounding so near.
A drink to my thirst, each vibrating note.
My vexing old burdens fall far remote.

"Then close your sad eyes. Your spirit regain.
Behold what fantastic symbols abound,
What wondrous host of cosmos around.
From silvery sand, the tiniest grain
To man and the planet, God's at the heart.
In shifting mosaic, souls doth impart.
His spirits who pass through multiformed earth
Some lesson of life must learn in each birth."

Divinely the Voice sang. I felt refreshed.
And vanished the night, abyss and despair.
Harmonious kinship made all things fair.
I yearned with my soul to venture unleashed.
Sweet Freedom. There stood in waiting, a steed
All prancing, well bridled, saddled for speed.
A foot in the stirrup! Off with a bound!
As light as a feather, making no sound.

Through ether, long leagues we galloped away.
An angry red river, we shyed in dismay,
For here were men sacrificed (cruel deed)
To reptiles and monsters, war, graft, and greed.
A jungle of discord drops in the rear.
By silence is quelled suspicious old fear,

And spite-gnats' low buzz is muffled at last.
Exploring the spirit, I must ride fast.

Away from these worldly ones, let us go,
Along a worn trail, much traveled and—Lo!
Familiar the scenes that come rushing by.
Now billowy sea and now azure sky.
Amid that enchanted spade, as they spun
Sun, moon, and the stars, their own orbits run!
Great Spirit, in realms so infinite reigns;
And wonderful wide are all His domains.

Hark! Here in the Spirit-world, He doth hold
A village of Indians, camped as of old.
Earth-legends by their fires, some did review,
While flowers and trees more radiant grew.
"Oh, You were all dead! In Lethe[1] you were tossed!"
I cried, "Every where 'twas told you were lost!
Forsooth, they did scan your footprints on sand.
Bereaved, I did mourn your fearful sad end."

Then spoke One of the Spirit Space, so sedate.
"My child, We are souls, forever and aye.
The signs in our orbits point us the way.
Like planets, we do not tarry nor wait.
Those memories dim, from Dust to the Man,
Called Instincts, are trophies won while we ran.
Now various stars where loved ones remain
Are linked to our hearts with Memory-chain."

"In journeying here, the Aeons we've spent
Are countless and strange. How well I recall
Old Earth trails: the River Red;[2] above all
The Desert sands burning us with intent.
All these we have passed to learn some new thing.
Oh hear me! Your dead doth lustily sing!
'Rejoice! Gift of Life pray waste not in wails!
           The maker of Souls forever prevails!'"

Direct from the Spirit-world came my steed.
The phantom has place in what was all planned.
He carried me back to God and the land
Where all harmony, peace and love are the creed.
In triumph, I cite my Joyous return.
The smallest wee creature I dare not spurn.
I sing "Gift of Life, pray waste not in wails!
The Maker of Souls forever prevails!"

American Indian Magazine 4 (1916): 57–59.

The Red Man's America

*In this poem, alternate lyrics to "My Country 'Tis of Thee,"
Zitkala-Ša refers to two pieces of legislation. Harry Lane (1855–
1917) was a democratic senator from Oregon (1913–17) who filed
numerous bills to abolish the Indian Bureau. Representative H. L.
Gandy (1881–1957), a democrat from South Dakota, introduced
1916 federal legislation to prohibit peyote use. It was defeated.
The music for "God Save the King" is from* Thesaurus Musicus
*(London, 1744). The lyrics to "My Country 'Tis of Thee" were
written by Samuel F. Smith in 1831.*

My country! 'tis to thee,
Sweet land of Liberty,
My pleas I bring.
>   Land where OUR fathers died,
>   Whose offspring are denied
>   The Franchise given wide,
>   Hark, while I sing.

My native country, thee,
Thy Red man is not free,
Knows not thy love.
>   Political bred ills,
>   Peyote in temple hills,
>   His heart with sorrow fills,
>   Knows not thy love.

Let Lane's Bill swell the breeze,
And ring from all the trees,
Sweet freedom's song.

Let Gandy's Bill awake
All people, till they quake,
Let Congress, silence break,
The sound prolong.

Great Mystery, to thee,
Life of humanity,
To thee, we cling.
Grant our home land be bright,
Grant us just human right,
Protect us by Thy might,
Great God, our king.

American Indian Magazine 5 (1917): 64.

A Sioux Woman's Love for Her Grandchild

To this historical poem, Zitkala-Ša added this note: "This incident occurred upon the coming of Custer's army, preliminary to the battle known erroneously in history as 'Custer's Massacre.'" That event took place June 25, 1876.

Loosely clad in deerskin, dress of flying fringes
Played a little black haired maiden of the prairies;
Plunged amid the rolling green of grasses waving.
Brimming o'er with laughter, round face all aglowing.
Thru the oval teepee doorway, grandma watched her,
Narrowed aged eyes reflecting love most tender.

Seven summers since a new-born babe was left her.
Death had taken from her teepee her own daughter.
Tireless love bestowed she on the little Bright eyes—
Eagerly attended her with great devotion.
Seven summers grew affection intertwining.
Bent old age adorned once more with hopes all budding.

Bright Eyes spied some "gaudy-wings" and
    chased them wildly.
Sipping dew and honey from the flowers, gaily
Flit the pretty butterflies, here now, then yonder.
"These the green, wee babes," old grandma mused in wonder.
"One time snug in winter slumber, now in season
Leave their silken cradles; fly with gauzy pinion."

Shouting gleefully, the child roamed on fearlessly
Glossy, her long hair, hung in two braids o'er each ear.
Zephyrs whispered to the flowers, at her passing.
Fragrant blossoms gave assent with gracious nodding.

Conscious lay the crystal dew, on bud and leaflet.
Iridescent joys, emitting till the sun set.

Monster clouds crept in the sky; fell shadows in the prairie
Grandma, on her cane, leaned breathless, sad and weary.
Listened vainly for the laughter of her darling.
"Where, Oh where, in sudden desert's endless rolling,
Could the wee girl still be playing?" cried she hoarsely,
Shaking as with ague in that silence somber.

Sobbing bitterly, she saw not men approaching.
Over-wrought by sorrow, scarcely heard them talking.
Gusts of wind by; cooled her fever;
Loosed her wisps of hair befitting to a mourner.
"In God's infinitude, where, Oh where is grandchild?"
Winds caught up her moaning, shrieked and shook the teepee.

"Dry your tears, old grandma, cease excessive wailing."
(Empty words addressed they to an image standing.)
"Chieftain's word of sympathy and warning, hear you!
Moving dust cloud of an army is on-coming;
Though you've lost your grandchild, tempt no useless danger.
In the twilight, we must flee hence." This the order.

Duty done, they paused with heads bowed sadly.
These strong men were used to meeting battles bravely,
Yet the anguish of the woman smote them helpless.
Setting of the sun made further searching fruitless,
Darkness, rife with evil omens surging tempest
Came, obliterating hope's last ray for rescue.

Fleeing from the soldiers startled Red Men hurried
Riding travois, ponies faced the lightnings, lurid
'Gainst the sudden flashing, angry fires, a figure
Stood, propped by a cane. A soul in torture
Sacrificing life than behind her lost one.
Greater love hath no man,[1] love surpassing reason.

American Indian Magazine 5 (1917): 230–31.

The Sun Dance Opera

William F. Hanson and Zitkala-Ša. Photographer unknown.
Gertrude and Raymond Bonnin Collection [MSS 1704]. Courtesy
of L. Tom Perry Special Collections, Harold B. Lee Library,
Brigham Young University, Provo, Utah.

In 1913, Bonnin's collaboration with William F. Hanson to create The Sun Dance Opera *returned her to the creative and public stage. Together, the two composed a work based on the Plains Sun Dance, a sacred ritual that had also been adapted by the Utes in Utah, where both composers lived. Although the basic framework of the opera incorporates the sacred vow of the Sun Dancers, the particular prayers and rituals are omitted.*

Bonnin's extraction from reservation life to live at a boarding school is well documented in her own published writings. As she attended these schools, surely she was also exposed to and trained in Christian hymnody. By the time she arrived at Earlham College in 1896, she was sufficiently trained in music to perform publicly: a vocal duet, a vocal solo, and a piano solo, Rondo Brilliante *by Weber. In 1899 she left her teaching post at the Carlisle Industrial Training School to study with a violinist at the New England Conservatory of Music in Boston. One of her most prestigious performances was a violin solo at the White House in 1900 for President William McKinley. At that occasion she also recited Longfellow's* Song of Hiawatha *(various issues of* The Earlhamite*).*

*Clearly part of the assimilating process of the Indian boarding schools was the inclusion of music in the curriculum. Not only did music represent a component of the historic university quadrivium/trivium structure of general education, it also inculcated an artistic hierarchy and religious ideology. As British author William Congreve proclaimed, "Music hath charms to soothe the savage breast, / To soften rocks, or bend a knotted oak" (*The Mourning Bride *1.1). Ironically, Bonnin, and undoubtedly others, responded well to the music curriculum because of the ways music is not culturally specific. Music is abstract and does not require language proficiency; music is greater than the sum of its parts; it is more than pitch, melody, harmony, and rhythm, and those elemental parts, in some ways, are not bound by culture. However, when the musical elements are ordered in particular ways, they do represent cultural phenomena, even ideology. On a personal level, Bonnin's musical performance provided validation and affirmation in an environment wherein she was culturally fractured.*

Young Gertrude Simmons saw herself as an artist. In March 1901 she was on her way from Boston back to South Dakota. Her book, Old Indian Legends, *had just been published, and her magazine articles were forthcoming in national periodicals. In a letter to Dr. Carlos Montezuma, later her fiancé, she contrasted her own sensibilities with his concrete, scientific approach. She writes: "I do not care about a doctor's profession more than those of the others. In truth music, art and literature are more in line with my own" (March 1901). She left the public life of eastern artistic cultural centers to return to South Dakota. She wrote Montezuma that her purpose for returning home was to gather and publish more stories. While working at odd jobs and trying to write, she also gave a piano performance at the Fort Totten school in June 1901.*

After her marriage to Raymond Bonnin, their conversion to Catholicism, and their move to Utah, apparently Gertrude Bonnin continued efforts in her music and discovered a fellow Catholic in a music class she taught in 1911. During the 1913 trip to the Midwest to place her son, Ohiya, in a Catholic boarding school she apparently took the time for some piano studies in Ohio. She writes in a letter to Montezuma: "I studied piano music at Otterbein University. I practised 6 hours a day. Now that's hard labor[.] I want to earn a diploma in Piano Music some of these days" (June 23, 1913).

Her music interests continued when she returned to Utah. In the evenings, local friends and neighbors would join in parlor performances. Participants included the Bonnins, Indian Bureau financial clerk Asa Chapman, and music teacher William F. Hanson. Hanson and Bonnin decided to collaborate on the composition of an opera with a local topic. They settled on the topic of the Sun Dance set against an appropriately romantic love triangle between Sioux maid Winona, Sioux hero Ohiya, and the evil Shoshone Sweet Singer. According to Hanson, Bonnin would play Sioux melodies on the violin and he would transcribe them. Then they would add harmonies and lyrics.

This process invites several levels of translation and removal from original source materials. In reading about indigenous musics in the terminology of mainstream culture, one learns that these musics are based in nonmetrical rhythmic patterns, pentatonic modes with occasional nonstandard pitches, vocables rather than lyrics, and nonharmonic melody patterns. In other words, traditional American Indian music is what Western civilization music is not and vice versa. What they have in common is cultural representation and performance. American Indian musics, however, stem from oral tradition and its characteristics. In oral tradition, not only is performance mutable, but the origins themselves may also be dynamic as one performer learns from another. Western music, although occasionally oral, tends to be literate and codified, with tempered scales, precise notations, and regulated and discrete meters. While the performance itself may be transitory, the music manuscript is fixed and permanent.

As Bonnin made the musical transition from traditional Sioux melodies to her version of grand opera, the process was a little like forcing a proverbial square peg into a round hole. She had the musical cognition to convert the vocal melodies to the violin. The nonfretted neck of the instrument could allow for the tonal subtleties outside the tempered scalar system. However, by the time Hanson committed the melodies to the fixed pitch system of the keyboard, along with the formulas of manuscript, the original indigenous melodies had been rendered unrecognizable. Add unimaginative harmonies that rarely exceed a secondary dominant and tom-tom rhythms and the result is what would sound to modern listeners like a soundtrack for a Western B movie. To the collaborators, Bonnin and Hanson, though, their creation was imaginative, and it was locally well received.

Part of the success of The Sun Dance Opera *was the incorporation of local Ute performers. At various times, the opera would come to a dead halt as the Native performers entered the stage to sing and dance. Because the Utes practiced the Sun Dance, it is easy to draw the conclusion that, knowing the topic, they performed their own ritualistic songs and dances. These set pieces are not scored in the opera.*

Additionally, certain structural elements in characters and themes of the opera reflect the Sun Dance and other cultural elements. For example, the opening piece has Shoshone Sweet Singer planning to use a love charm to magically win the devotion of Winona. Love medicines as manifestations of traditional beliefs are merely one cultural aspect of the opera. Others are footnoted in the libretto.

The basic plot of the opera unfolds around the Sun Dance vow of the hero, Ohiya. He sets out to win the heart of Winona. His intertribal rival is Sweet Singer. Secondary characters such as Blue Necklace, Gossips, and Hebo (the Heyoka or contrary) come to Ohiya's aid. The Sun Dance arena is set up, and Winona and Ohiya declare their love for each other. They bid the evil influences of the Witches to stay away.

Winona's father, the Chieftain, has the power to choose her husband. He is swayed by the lavish gifts of Sweet Singer. However, the discarded lover, Shoshone Maiden, comes to confront Sweet Singer, who momentarily expresses regret for bewitching her but then viciously promises to make Ohiya suffer in the Sun Dance. If Ohiya weakens from Sweet Singer's long songs, Winona will be lost. The scene shifts to the Sun Dance and invocations. Shoshone Maid vows to take Sweet Singer to the Pipestone Quarry. As the Sun Dance is enacted, Ohiya fulfills his vow and wins Winona.

The motivations behind the composition and performances of The Sun Dance Opera *are complex and layered in Hanson's colonial admiration for American Indians and Bonnin's desires to validate her own cultural her-*

itage. Hanson went on to claim the opera as his own. Later, during his distinguished career as a music professor at Brigham Young University, he revived the opera. It was performed in New York City as Opera of the Year in 1938, to disappointing reviews.

In 1914 Bonnin left Utah to enter the national scene of American Indian politics, fighting for causes that would consume the remainder of her life. There is no record that she had any association with the opera when it was revived. She died in Washington DC before its actual performance in 1938. There is virtually no mention of music in the surviving documentation from her later life.

Sample of The Sun Dance Opera. *Gertrude and Raymond Bonnin collection [MSS 1704]. Courtesy of L. Tom Perry Special Collections, Harold B. Lee Library, Brigham Young University, Provo, Utah.*

The Sun Dance Opera

Overture and Prologue

CHANT

Sweet Singer: There surely is a virtue in the love leaves. I gave her the love leaves, but I do not want her. How can I rid myself of her? How can I hide the shame of stealing from our medicine men, the sacred love leaves, charm leaves.

Disgraced, when they see her close beside me. I gave her the love leaves, but I do not want her, the powerful charm has blinded her. She stays beside me. Oh shame for stealing from our medicine man, the sacred love leaves, charm leaves.

I'll leave my land for the Sioux, for the Sioux! I'll leave my land! I'll join the Sioux! I'll leave my land! I'll join the Sioux! Forgetting my past days, seeking new friends.

I'll hie to the land of the Sioux, remembering only the songs of my people; I'll fly to the land of the Sioux, of the Sioux, the SIOUX.

Act I

Winona *(chanting)*: I met him whom I love. He smiled with his eyes. He smiled at me with love in his eyes. He smiled at me but I dared not reply.

Ohiya: Stay, a question I would ask thee. Answer truly dear Winona. Who this stranger at thy chieftain father's dwelling? Has he come to see thy father? Does he linger at thy teepee? Singing Sun Dance songs all vainly for Winona.

Winona: The Sweet Singer is the Shoshone, a stranger in our village now made welcome at our teepee by my brother.
Nightly sings the Sun Dance music he.[1] Sweet Singer the Shoshone, with his singing he has captured my dear father.

DUET

Winona: On words from Ohiya I ponder what rumors will reach him, I wonder. ART THOU BLIND TO LOVE I BEAR THEE? WHAT WORDS THESE OHIYA, BRAVE OHIYA, HOW COULD'EST THOU DOUBT ME? PRAY Let me idle gossip turn thee; no gossip boastful stranger disturb thy heart.

Ohiya: He is guest to her young brother. Guest only to her, to her young brother. Slyly eyeing thee, that bold knave.

Winona: Friend to all is he. Yet 'tis I who truly love thee. I truly love thee with all my heart.

DUET: LOVE IS FOR VALOR

Ohiya: Beware of Sweet Singer, a man of idle thoughts. Love is for valor, not for empty words. I will not throw my love away. Adore the brave and true. Throw not love away. I love the brave and true. I love the true.

Winona: Beware of Sweet Singer, a man with idle thoughts. Love is for valor, not for empty words. Throw not to him your love away. Give only to the true heed one brave to do. Love but the brave and true, I love but you.

Winona (*chanting*): I stand in the West. I beckon come to me.

Ohiya: Inkpata Nawaze Naci, Naci, coze May Maya Leci cu wana.[2]

THE VOW

Ohiya: What love was in her tender eye, and yet she, she could not not conceal it.

Winona *(from afar)*: I stand in the West. I beckon come to me.

WE WILL LOVE HIM

Blue Necklace and Gossips

Blue Necklace: If this be true about Sweet Singer leave.

Gossips: What shall we do?[3]

Blue Necklace: That to me and you shall see, for I've a scheme—I'll tell you—to rid our tribe of this Shoshone.

Gossips: Rid of Shoshone, Oh could she? How?

Blue Necklace: Yes! I'll steal his love from Winona.

Gossips: From Winona, she'll do it.

Blue Necklace: I will. I need but one assistant only. Give Hebo. Crazy he is and steal his love. See our plan will be to rid of him, to free our tribe of this. Let us now try Sweet Singer.

Gossips: Let us now try till he shall, till he shall die. Blue Necklace here, and Hebo to rid of him. We will die—Blue Necklace here, and Hebo to rid our tribe of him to rid of him. We will love him—tease and please him, scare and haunt him—day and night—till his life here be a burden, till he leaves us here in peace. We will love him. We will tease him. We will please him the Shoshone. We will care him; we will haunt him. O with him away. Away with Shoshone.

Sweet Singer: Winona, Winona! I'll give the sacred love potions from the Shoshone. She now come to me, to me.

Gossips: We'll love him, tease and please him . . .

Sweet Singer: Winona, Winona! I hied to the land of the Sioux.

Hebo:[4] He thinks that I'm Winona! And as I'm Winona. I bid you serenade. Were you wooing? I thought I heard a howling coyote. You bring our Sioux people bad luck, thus wooing. O Ho! Did you hear that about Running Bird?

Sweet Singer: Running Bird?

Hebo (*pinching* Sweet Singer's *ear*): You must never mention the name of your mother-in-law, or a pinched ear![5] Don't you know that Running Bird is the mother of Blue Necklace whom you were just courting?

Wan! (Wa!) My friend—

My companion here and I had given you up. We waited for long time at one chieftain's lodge for you. Did you not tell us this day you would teach us some of the Sun Dance songs?

Sweet Singer (*glad for a relief excuse*): Yes, yes. I'll get my drum. (*Exits assisted by two of* Hebo's *friends*)

HEBO

Hebo Hebo Hebo Hebo. The lazy the crazy, eternally stubborn Hebo—

Hebo Hebo Hebo Hebo.

The lazy, the crazy eternally stubborn Hebo Hebo.

My name? My name is Hebo.

Your yes, my contrary no.

To run, for me is to stand

To swim, for me is to land.

No Yes No Yes Yes No No Yes No.

Your yes, my contrary no.

Your tears laugh I away
I turn dull toil into play.
So contrary am I, tho scalped I could not die.
I hate to hunt buffalo.
They cried, "Run Eastward, Hebo."
West I turned and ran into the foe.
To run, for me is to stand
To swim, for me is to land.
When you ask, "Is the water deep?"
"Drown me yourself," I reply.
So contrary am I,
tho scalped I could not die.
The lazy, the crazy, yet praiseworthy, stubborn Hebo.

MONOLOGUE

Yet when alone, Yet when alone, I think about my self—
my real self. So no I look at him my self. So no I look at me
my own self stares at me. I know him now, he that is weak.
He wearies when others falter not. His breath quickly
chokes. His heart beats hard and loud. When others rise,
when others rise he winks. My really-self fails. His head is
drooping. His face draws cold. He gazes listlessly at me. His
fingers clinch his eyes. They stare as ghostly now, his fingers creep toward me slowly like spirits to devour me. His
evil eye is haunting me. He's come to kill me. Ho. No, I'm
Hebo, only he the lazy the crazy eternally stubborn Hebo.

Sweet Singer *(returning with his tom-tom)*: Come, now to the
Sun Dance songs.

MALE CHORUS

HI . . . Hi. . . HO! My friend, never kill a spider,
never kill a spider without say.[6] Grandfather thunder

killed you. Bad luck. Grandfather thunders out. Yes, bad luck for you. Come now to the Sun Dance. Come the Sun Dance songs to sing. HO! Did you hear that story. What a story?

Discordant practices. Sweet Singer *attempts to teach the stubborn (seemingly half-witted)* Hebo *the Sun Dance songs. But in this short period of real Indian experience, the amused* Chorus, *led by* Blue Necklace *and the Gossips, enters and form a semicircle behind the singers.*

Hebo (*stopping the song*): A Sioux took a Shoshone friend for a buffalo hunt. Both were mounted on fleet-footed ponies. They had not ridden far when they came upon a great old buffalo. The wounded buffalo made a sudden fierce charge at the horsemen. The alert Sioux made his escape, but the Shoshone's horse was gored to death! Shoshone! Ha, ha!

Sweet Singer (*pounding the tom-tom*): Let us practice! (*Sweet Singer, embarrassed by the laughing crowd of onlookers, starts to leave. He crosses in front of* Hebo, *who halts him.*)

Hebo: Don't do that! You give me bad luck. Don't you know that you should never cross in front of one man when the wind is blowing from the north? Never pass between the north wind and a dear friend like Hebo![7] (*As* Sweet Singer *leaves, the contrary one and his companions follow him.*)

Hebo (*strutting while the crowd laughs*): Wan! My friend. Bad luck seems to be following you, Sweet Singer. (Blue Necklace *joins* Hebo.) Ho! Now hear now my story. Hebo Hebo Hebo Hebo. The lazy, the crazy, eternally stubborn Hebo Hebo.

Crier:[8] Ho! Tribesmen all, our chieftain comes. He call hi yi! So list' to our leader's wish. Hi Ho yi Hi yi you Hi yi you, chieftain comes. Hi list' to chieftain's word. Hi yi yi Hi yi yi Hi yi you Hi you HI yi.

Chief Crier: Why now? Why now? Why now? Why linger here? You linger at morn. We must away to our circle. Our chieftain comes with word. Circle, circle camping Sun Dance land under pipestone cliffs.[9] Hi yi hi you. Why linger here? For at camp Sun Dance land, pipestone cliffs a way hi you! Why linger here? For at pipestone cliffs. Morn we must away to worship Schenawv[10] spirit so away, away. Hi to worship Schenawv. Great spirit away away Hi yi I. Away to circle camp away. Hie to Sun Dance land away away. Hie away, Hie away, Hie away!

Act II

INTRODUCTION: CHORUS CHANT, CIRCLE DANCE (SQUAW DANCE), SENZA ORCHESTRA

Crier: Ho! I call attention all for they come from the sham battle. These our braves with Sun Dance poles,[11] our braves' last captives.

Now make way that they may join in the story, one and all. Each to tell his deed of bravery our braves in battle. OHIYA BRAVE; HE LEADS THEM ALL.[12]

Chorus: Ohiya Brave! He leads them all. Honor the victor of the field. Ohiya Brave, our praises call now all foes to him shall be heard. Yield to Ohiya, Ohiya Brave. *("Sham Battle" staged)*

THE TALL TREES (BASS & CHORUS)

Chant: The Tall Trees The Tall Trees. The Tall Trees captured for our Sun Dance Ground, Tall Trees captured for our Sun Dance Grounds. Mediator to Schenawv, Mediator to Schenawv. Arms of trees ever uplifted to Schenawv, arms of trees ever uplifted to Schenawv, Schenawv.

Tall Trees captured for our Sun Dance Grounds, Tall Tree

with arms ever uplifted to Schenawv, to Schenawv, Schenawv. The Tall Trees ever wave and sway in perpetual worship to Schenawv. Pray in worship to Schenawv. Now our braves they dance to Schenawv. *(chant and whistle)*

Dance and worship five days and nights as they dance in Sun Dance, worship in Sun Dance prayer. *(chant)*

All braves now dance to fill these vows. The Tall Trees. Braves now dance to fill sacred vows. The Tall Trees, Tall Trees captured for our Sun Dance Ground.

Braves vow Chieftain's dance to great Schenawv. *(chant)*

WAR DANCE

(Male singers chant)

Act III

SERENADE TO WINONA WITH INDIAN FLUTE

Ohiya: Inkpata Nawaze Naci, Naci, coze May Maya Leci cu wana.[13]

Winona: (I stand. . . .)

Ohiya *(chanting)*: I'll win Winona for a bride, she whom the proudest chief could pride. Winona, Winona, Winona for a bride, Winona, Winona, Winona, Winona for a bride.

Winona: I come to you. Oh come to me.

Ohiya's Serenade: I stand in the West. I beckon come to me. Inkpata Nawaze Naci, Naci, coze May Maya Leci cu wana.

Winona: Hark! The Call of Ohiya. It is my love. It is my love. It is my love. He smiled at me with love in his eyes; he smiled at me but I dared not reply.

Ohiya *(in background)*: I'll win Winona for my bride.

Winona: My love! So when he calls to me to me I answer. I stand in the west and beckon come to me, come to . . .

Ohiya *(in background)*: Inkpata Nawaze Naci, Naci, coze May Maya Leci cu wana.

Winona: Through the magic of the moonlight comes the call of the serenade.

Braves: List' the call of the serenade, serenade.

Ohiya: Winona for a bride, she whom the proudest chief could pride. Winona, Winona, I'll win Winona for a bride; I'll win with love in deeds of bravery my bride *(Winona simultaneously echoes words)*

MEN'S CHORUS, OHIYA, AND WINONA REPEAT

Winona (monologue): I heard the love notes of his flute, and his voice echoing along the live moonbeams!

O! The night of charm! The moonlight magic!

Ohiya! My Ohiya! My Serenade!

The magic of the night steals upon me.

A wonder world you reign upon, O gentle Moon.

Yes! it turns to a fairy-world the most familiar trees and foothills.

O fairy Indian people—People of the night world, hear me, I pray to you.—[14]

Aid my lover in his great test for me, for he has vowed.

At the Sun Dance, give him courage—give him strength, for it is a great test.

Yon fields of the firefly lands,

I recall my childhood fright lest your crop of winged cinder should burn me in their flight.

Send your myriad sparks to hover over the elfin arrowhead makers.

Cast your lights on their tiny ticking chisels that they may the better perfect the magic arrowhead for Ohiya.

Of our braves on your high walls, thus dooming them to untimely death.

I have heard HOW one of our braves declared he wished to marry one of the Witches of the Night,[15] and HOW that very night, you carved his form.

On the morrow he lay cold in death.

You had called him to your land of Spirits and of Witches.

O Witches of the Pipestone Quarry, do not beguile Ohiya from me.

Do not take him away.

And you tiny elfin arrowhead makers—Make for my love the arrowhead of the crystal flint.

Shape for him the choicest arrowheads.

Put magic into them, that in his hunt Ohiya shall never fail.

And you, little stars, and big stars,

I have heard HOW you were once young braves and old warriors who have gone to the Wonder-world.

Pray look kindly down upon Ohiya.

Sometimes come to him in a vision. Show him the wonders you hold so securely, in your high skyland.

I heard the love notes of his flute and his voice echoing along the silver moonbeams.

O tiny fairy Indian people, who work and play mid moonlight magic,

O fairies of the night world, hear me and aid my lover in his great test.

WINONA'S ARIA: THE MAGIC OF THE NIGHT

The magic of the Night of Nights beckons me

A wonder-world is shelter 'neath the trees.

From grass and shrubs and willows low

Come mystic voices, sighs enchanting breeze.

The pallid lake lies quiet now

Beneath yon mountain's somber breath.

The moonlight flickers—branches bow

But I? My lover comes! He comes to me!

Oh night of nights!

He comes—in his serenade!

Before the coyote's call at morn,

Or bird awakes its mate at dawn,

While mystic voices sing their song

He comes—my lover comes—I know 'tis he!

Ohiya, yes Ohiya Brave—in his serenade.

I pass into the nightworld unafraid.

He comes to chant ecstasy

He comes to chant his serenade.

(She hears the serenade of Ohiya's *flute.)*

TO THE WITCHES OF THE NIGHT

Winona: To the Witches of the Night when no man, no man
hath seen you who carve on pipestone at night. At night
so keen . . . Oh leave no pictures of our braves. Their forms
let not, let not us see. Let not us see with the fate. Do not
come. Do not come to enchant our braves. Do not chip on
the cliff. Oh make not a picture of fate. Stay away. Stay
away. Oh! make not a picture of fate. Stay away, lest we die
away, away. Make no picture of our braves; stay away.

Winona and Chorus: But the fairies lithe and small friend to us in time of need you. On man good luck bestow. You live 'mongst grass and trees making arrows for our braves. By light by light of your firefly birds (your firefly birds) chip away, chip away, making magic arrow points; chip away, chip away, making arrows till the day; chip away, chip away, good luck on our braves bestow. Chip away, lest we die (away, away) making magic arrow points for our braves.

THE SERENADE

Ohiya *(singing vow)*: Inkpata Nawaze Naci, Naci, coze May Maya Leci cu wana.

Winona: The magic of the night of nights beckons me, beckons me, beckons me; a wonder-world is sheltered 'neath the trees from grass and shrub and willows low. Come mystic voices, sighs, enchanting breeze from mystic voices, sighs enchanting breeze. The pallid lake lies quiet now beneath your mountain's somber breast. The moonlight? Branches low but I, but I, my lover comes, he comes to me of night, of night, he comes to me in his serenade.

Before the coyotes call at morn or bird awakes its mate dawn while spirits mystic sing their song he come he come come. My love comes I know 'tis he.

Ohiya brave, Ohiya brave. I know 'tis he; know that it is he. In the serenade my love comes to sing to me, comes to sing his serenade.

I pass into the night world unafraid. He comes to chant, O ecstasy, he comes to chant his serenade.

Hark, the voice of my love. Hark, the voice of Ohiya. It is my love *(repeat)*. Hark, the voice of my lover.

Ohiya: I stand in the west.

Winona: My lover, the serenade; I met him but I dared not reply.

Ohiya: I stand in the west. I beckon come to me.

Winona: He smiled at me with love in his eyes. He smiled at me but I dared not reply.

Ohiya: I'll win Winona for a bride.

Winona: When he calls, when he calls, I answer, I stand, I beckon, I stand in the west.

Winona and Ohiya: I beckon come to me.

Ohiya: Inkpata Nawaze Naci, Naci, coze May Maya Leci cu wana.

Winona and Ohiya: Through the magic of the moonlight comes the call of the serenade.

Winona: I come to you Ohiya brave *(chants . . .)*

Ohiya: List' the call of the serenade. I'll win Winona for a bride. She whom the wealth of worlds could pride. Winona, Winona, I'll win Winona for my bride. O win with love in deed of bravery.

Winona: Ohiya

Ohiya: Winona

Male Chorus: He wins Winona for a bride, she whom the wealth of world could pride. Winona, Winona, Winona for a bride, Winona, Winona, Winona for a bride, an Indian bride, an Indian bride.

TO THE WITCHES OF THE NIGHT—CHORAL DUET

To the Witches of the Night whom no man, no man, hath seen. You, who come on pipestone height at night with eyes so keen, leave no picture of our braves, their forms. Let not us see, let not us see, with thy fate. Do not come, do not come to enchant our braves. Do not chip on the cliff or make not a picture of fate; stay away, stay away. O make not a picture of fate. Stay away, let me away making magic arrow points for our braves. But the fair lithe and small friends to us in time of need, for on man good luck bestow. You live amongst grass and reeds making arrows for our braves by light the night of your firefly birds, your firefly birds. Man chips away making magic arrow points, chip away, chip away making arrows till the day; chip away, chip away, good luck on our braves bestow; chip away lest we stay away.

Act IV

Shoshone Maid: I fled the rule of modesty; why did you leave me?

Sweet Singer: I'll leave my land, I'll leave my land, for the Sioux, for the Sioux. I'll leave my land, I'll leave my land, for the Sioux. I'll leave my land I'll from the Sioux.

Shoshone Maid: I was so lonely without your singing; would not endure your absence, could not, but follow you.

Sweet Singer: The powerful charm has blinded her; she stays beside me for stealrous [?] from the medicine men, the sacred love leaves.

Sweet Singer: Leave my land; I'll leave my land.

Shoshone Maid: I was so weary; I wandered through the wilderness only to be with you, only to be with you, to be with you. Come to me when I grow faint from hunger and fatigue. All nature exhorted me to persevere; the flowers nodded their heads, birds sent to me, told me yet I would find you. At last I have found you; tell me what I yearn to hear. Say you are happy to see me.

Sweet Singer (*repeating over Shoshone Maid*): I'll leave my land; I'll join the Sioux.

Shoshone Maid: I was so lonely. O come to me, O come to me. Only to be with thee, only to be with thee, to be with thee, come to me, to me. Sweet Singer, you leave me yet again? You leave me for another, desert me again? No, it cannot be, it must not be, it will not be, for I will make a vow and a prayer to win him. I vow to all Indians, to Shoshone, to the Sioux, I vow to the Witches of the Night, to immortal which is of the Pipestone Quarry; I vow even unto death. He shall come to for an immortal charm. Incur I death; He shall come. I will love him forever. He too shall die. He too shall die. He'll die to be with me. High on the cliff of the Pipestone Quarry his fated picture shall I carve upon the wall of the cliff. Sweet Singer, you'll come to me. The power, the charm of the love leaves. The power and charm of the love leaves have brought me hither. I've forsaken my tepee, defied the rules of modesty.

Long ago Shoshone maid was charmed by a singer with his songs and his love leaves. Her heart he won away. She will love him forever, will follow him always; she will love him forever, will follow him always, I follow.

But O my heart I must away. None else shall see me, none but my love shall know I am cured. I follow him always, not else to be loved. He must come back, my love, to me and soothe my aching heart.

(DIALOGUE INSERT)

Chieftain *(entering)*: Daughter, I come to this sacred place to pray for wisdom. My heart is troubled. I would choose the ablest man for you to wed.

Winona: Father, there is not doubt. There is only one to choose for me.

Chieftain: Daughter, I cannot be swayed by your childish fancy. I must choose with the mature heart of a parent. Whether he be singer or dancer, the great eagle shall signify to me. The eagle, who soars to loftiest heights to commune with Schenawv, the wonder-bird who also scans the hearts of man, the great eagle, wisest of all, shall testify. He will reveal the answer to our prayers and to our dreams. I pray I may choose aright.

GREAT EAGLE (CHIEFTAIN'S PRAYER)

Chieftain: Great Eagle Down from your heights descend. Thou kind of the sky with keen unerring eye, unerring eye, scanned the hearts of men who as suitor vie to win Winona. Hi hi ji a hi I I I hi I.

Great Eagle, when Wacipi[16] ends appear o'er his head and shout to name the man, the truest one, bravest of all those who as suitors vow to win Winona.

Pray hover o'er the bravest one, whom deeds make worthy to be my son, whom deeds make worthy to be my son, and win Winona my daughter dear. HI HI ui hi hi I hi I hi I I hi hi I Hi ihi hi ya.

(DIALOGUE INSERT)

Messenger: Chieftain! I have this day taken to your dwelling, a pony laden with rich gifts. They are from Sweet Singer . . . Chieftain, the Shoshone brave asks for your daughter.

Chieftain: Go, my friend. Tell your Shoshone brave I shall bear him in mind. At the close of the Sun Dance, within the very arena, I shall give my daughter to him who answers my requirements of a man.

Sweet Singer *(to* Winona*):* From whence do you bring those sweet herbs? For whom did you gather them? Ah, you need not confess it. They are for your love, your lover?"

(Winona starts to leave. Sweet Singer grabs the love leaves from her.)

Sweet Singer: Stay! Let me tell you what I shall bring as an offering for you, Ohiya brave. Since I am director of the Sun Dance music, I shall sing my longest songs for him to dance by. I will test his boasted endurance. Ha, ha! You say he won the footrace, that his pony outran mine, that his eye and arm are more steady in shooting the arrow. Ha, ha!

What are these? Child's play. Aye, and you shall be winless.

I will sing such long songs that Ohiya's strength shall be as naught. Before the fifth day of the ceremony, he shall be exhausted. He shall reel to and fro as a baby; his courage shall go with his strength. He shall fall. Your prayers, your green herbs, cannot save him! Down with the prayer herbs. His weakness in the holy Sun Dance shall be his undoing. Aye and you shall be witness. Then you will come to me.

(Singing resumes)

Sweet Singer: I gave her the love leaves. I must forget Shoshone. Gave her the love leaves but I do not want her. I do not want her; I do not want her. I fly to the land of the Sioux remembering only the love of my people. I fly to the land of the Sioux, of the Sioux, the Sioux. But now Winona, my Winona, my Winona, Winona, Winona, Winona, Winona, turned me coldly by; turned me coldly by. My love for another heart doth and today bare break will bring, will bring for him and there sweet heart will sway for him, it cannot be, it must not be. With my songs will I cruel heart win. It cannot be; it will not be. He shall be and stagger, fall in disgrace. My victim, my love shall be his disgrace. He shall fall, my victim. He shall weary stagger, weary stagger, faint and fall, shall fall my victim.

(DIALOGUE INSERT)

Sweet Singer: Five days and nights for him to dance! Five days in the burning sun! Where are the Sun Dance whistles? Where is Ohiya? Soon the struggle twixt him and me!

Hebo and Blue Necklace: Were you singing? I thought I heard a howling coyote. You are surely calling forth evil spirits for our Sun Dance! But why so sad? Are you about to chant your death song?

Sweet Singer: No, I am about to chant Ohiya's death time!

Blue Necklace: If you should need assistance, call upon Blue Necklace and the loveable Hebo Hinnu! Hinnu! Bad luck seems to be following you, Shoshone! Do you know, singer, that there is echo from your Shoshone people that their warriors are on the war path? They seek a certain Shoshone Maid! Do you know of her? Have you seen her? Is it abduction?

Hebo: Her betrayer should be shot with the poison arrows!

Blue Necklace: If the Sioux hear about her, what may they not do?

DUET: SHOSHONE MAID AND SWEET SINGER

Shoshone Maid: The power and charm of love leaves, the power and charm of love leaves, have brought me hither. I've forsaken my tepee, defied the rule of modesty, defied the rule of modesty. Why did you leave me?

Sweet Singer: I'll leave my land, I'll leave my land, for the SIOUX, for the SIOUX. I'll leave my land, I'll join the Sioux, I'll leave my land, I'll join the Sioux.

Shoshone Maid: I was so lonely without your singing, could not endure your absence, could not but follow you.

Sweet Singer: The powerful charm has blinded her. She stays beside me for stealing from the medicine men the sacred love leaves.

Shoshone Maid: I was so weary, I wandered through the wilderness.

(both)

Shoshone Maid: Oh come to me, oh come to me, oh come to me.

Sweet Singer: I'll leave my land, I'll leave my land, for the Sioux.

Shoshone Maid: When I grew faint from hunger and fatigue, all nature exhorted me to persevere. The flowers nodded their heads, birds sent to me told me yet I would find you. At last I have found you; tell me what I yearn to hear. Say you are happy to see me.

Shoshone Maid: Sweet Singer, you leave me yet again? You leave me for another? Desert me? Again? No it cannot be, it must not be, for I will make a vow and a prayer to win him. I vow to all Indians, to Shoshone, to the Sioux. I vow, to the Witches of the Night, to immortal Witches of the Pipestone Quarry, I vow even unto death! He shall come to me for an immortal charm. In cruel death, he shall come. He will love me forever. He too shall die. He'll die, he'll die, to be with me. High on the cliff of the Pipestone Quarry, his fatal picture shall I carve. Sweet Singer will come.

SUNSET MARCH

Shoshone Maid: FORSAKEN. Lonely words in hunted forests, my heart sobs with your cry. Plaintive eaglet in your nest, my heart is famished, too. I will love him forever; I love him still. The Pipestone Quarry, let me be one of you, with immortal witchery his heart to win away. Then he'll love me forever; he'll die, die, die, he'll die for me that day.

SUN CALL

Unison Chorus (chanting):

GREAT SPIRIT HEAR OUR PRAYER

In this dance to Great Sun

To all who vow Give a Vision

To All who vow Give Endurance

O let them dance till a vision, Give a vision clear

O let them dance till a vision comes

Hear our prayer, Schenawv Hi

May none fall in disgrace, May none fall

O may none fall in disgrace, in disgrace,

Courage, Endurance, endurance to our braves

Hear our prayers

May none fall in disgrace, in disgrace

Hi yi in disgrace

Courage, endurance, endurance to our braves

Hear our vows Hi yi

Grant the wish of the lover, the lover, the lover

Grant the wish of the lover

Grant the prayer, Schenawv

Hear, Oh hear us Hi.

Sunset March

SUN DANCE

Ohiya: At set of sun, at set of sun.

Chorus *(chanting)*: At set of sun, at set of sun, O Wacipi is
begun. At set of sun, Wacipi is begun, Wacipi is begun.
The vows of braves to dance Wacipi. Five days Sun Dance
vowed. Five days of Great Sun Dance vowed. Vowed but
the trees, but the great tall trees, but the Sun Dance trees,
but Sun Dance trees are vowed by the great tall trees. Vow
and prayers to Schenawv, the sacred songs the Sun Dance
prayer.

(Chant and whistles)

TO GREAT SCHENAWV
MY LOVE OR BURNING SANDS ASLEEP

(simultaneous)

Winona: O green herbs now you keep, for lies my brave on the sand asleep. Long has he danced to eaglet's cry in summer's heat heavy by. But my love weary reels and falls but for you. Green herbs hear his calls, your life, my love, your courage heal.

Ohiya: So long ago was prayer begun to great Schenawv beyond the sun. Now dances heard endurance frail, I bring green herbs that cannot fail. Refreshment rare and strength to give that your brave may happy live your life, my love, your life, my love.

Act V: Sun Dance Arena Finale

#1 SUN DANCE NO ORCHESTRA
#2 SUN DANCE NO ORCHESTRA

At the close of this dance, Ohiya is taken to booth cover with a white robe, and he falls asleep.

Winona *(singing the aria at center pole)*: O green herbs, now you keep, for lies my brave on the sand asleep. Long has he danced to eaglet's cry in summer's heat heavy by. But my love, weary reels and falls but for you. Green herbs hear his calls, your life, my love, your courage heal.

Notes

Acknowledgments

1. As noted later, Zitkala-Ša is the self-given pen name of Gertrude Simmons Bonnin. Throughout this work I will refer to "Zitkala-Ša" when referencing her artistic creations and use "Bonnin" or "Simmons" in general reference.

2. At the time of this writing, Brigham Young University Special Collections was organizing the Bonnin Collection into a more accessible order. The folder and file references from my initial research are no longer applicable.

Introduction

1. Dexter Fisher, ed., *The Third Woman: Minority Women Writers of the United States* (Boston: Houghton, 1980); *The Norton Anthology of American Literature*, 4th ed., vol. 2 (New York: Norton, 1994), 877–905; Judith Fetterly and Marjorie Pryse, eds., *American Women Regionalists: A Norton Anthology* (New York: Norton, 1992), 532–63; Sandra M. Gilbert and Susan Gubar, eds., *The Norton Anthology of Literature by Women* (New York: Norton, 1996), 1310–13; Paul Lauter, ed., *The Heath Anthology of American Literature*, 2nd ed., vol. 2 (Lexington MA: Heath, 1994), 925–40; Linda Wagner-Martin and Cathy N. Davidson, eds., *The Oxford Book of Women's Writing in the United States* (New York: Oxford UP, 1995), 514–22; William L. Andrews, ed., *Classic American Autobiographies* (New York: Penguin, 1992); Eugenia DeLamotte, Natania Meeker, and Jean F. O'Barr, eds., *Women Imagine Change: A Global Anthology of Women's*

Resistance from 600 B.C.E. to Present (New York: Routledge, 1997), 148–51.

Interestingly, early anthologies of American Indian literature do not include Zitkala-Ša. Paula Gunn Allen reintroduces her in *Spider Woman's Granddaughters: Traditional Tales and Contemporary Writing by Native American Women* ([New York: Fawcett, 1990], 34–43) and *Voice of the Turtle: American Indian Literature, 1900–1970* ([New York: Ballantine, 1994], 184–98).

2. Agnes M. Picotte offers this translation of Ellen Simmons's name in her foreword to *Old Indian Legends.* The feminine suffix "Win" would suggest "Woman Who Reaches for the Wind" (xii).

3. Riggs's work was used by missionaries and in Bible translations. Consequently, the literacy of Dakota became widespread.

4. According to Craig Howe (Lakota), *Ša* is the ceremonial form of "red" and is closer to "scarlet." *Luta* also means "red" in Lakota.

5. Her most frequent correspondence was with Father William Ketchum and Father [?] Martin.

6. When editor of *American Indian Magazine*, Bonnin closed letters with this phrase.

Stories

1. The new pieces were "A Dream of Her Grandfather" and "The Widespread Enigma of the Blue-Star Woman." Bonnin also introduced "America's Indian Problem," largely a reprint of a 1915 report on the Bureau of Indian Affairs, published in *Edict Magazine*, author unknown but presumed to be Bonnin.

2. In a chapter in her dissertation, Alice Poindexter Fisher does a comparative textual analysis of Deloria and Zitkala-Ša's "Iktomi and the Ducks."

The Buffalo Woman

1. See also Julian Rice, *Lakota Storytelling* ([New York: Lang, 1989], 104–08), and the *Pte* cycle in James Walker's *Lakota Myth* (ed. Elaine Jahner [Lincoln: U of Nebraska P, 1983], 109–18; 245–89).

2. *Papa* and *wasna* are dried meat.

3. *Tagu* is literally "old bull." Possibly Bonnin is also doing a wordplay on *Taku Wakan,* a physical manifestation of *wakan,* or sacred power. See also DeMallie and Parks, *Sioux Indian Religion.*

4. The owl is very powerful in traditional Sioux culture. Its call at night may signify a ghost. The owl is also the warrior of *Unktehi.* See note 1 of "Buzzard Skin and the Sea Monsters."

When the Buffalo Herd Went West

1. For a discussion of gender complementarity among Plains groups, see Albers and Medicine, *The Hidden Half.*

2. See Andrew Wiget, "His Life in His Tail," in *Redefining American Literary History*, ed. A. LaVonne Brown Ruoff and Jerry W. Ward Jr. (New York: MLA, 1990), 83–96; Gerald Vizenor, *Narrative Chance: Postmodern Discourse on Native American Indian Literatures* (Albuquerque: U of New Mexico P, 1989); Paul Lauter, "The Literatures of America: A Comparative Discipline," in *Redefining American Literary History*, ed. A. LaVonne Brown Ruoff and Jerry W. Ward Jr. (New York: MLA, 1990), 9–35; Barbara Babcock-Abrahams, "A Tolerated Margin of Mess," *Journal of the Folklore Institute* 11.3 (1975): 147–86.

3. Iktomi is the Lakota trickster. In *Old Indian Stories*, Bonnin, as Zitkala-Ša, wrote a number of Iktomi trickster stories. She indicated that her audience was children, as the stories were used as socialization techniques to reinforce moral behavior.

Buzzard Skin and the Sea Monsters

1. At the turn of the twentieth century, James Walker was told about *Unktehi*: "*Unktehi* are like animals. They stay in the waters and live in the swampy places. They have four legs and horns which they can draw in or extend them to the skies. They have long hair on the neck and the head which is *wakan*. Their tails are strong and they can shoot or strike with them, and they use their tails as men use their hands. They are always at war with the *Wakinyan*. When they move they make the waves and they destroy all living things they can get hold of" (*Lakota Belief and Ritual*, 108).

2. *Shee* means "stop" or "be still."

The Stone Boy and the Grizzly

1. Bonnin's original typed text reads, "With his knife he disemboweled the grizzly." The change is in her handwriting.

2. *Wotawe* are sacred emblems.

3. *Koda* means a particular friend of a Dakota man.

4. *Na* is either imperative, "only," or an adverbial exclamation.

The Making of Thunder People

1. *Tahince-Iheya* perhaps means "deer-shot."

The Witch Woman

1. *Inhan! Inhan!* is "Surely! Surely!"

Squirrel Man and His Double

1. Telephone interview, June 18, 1998.

Prayer of Pe-Šnija—Shriveled-Top

1. "*Tiošpaye*, which generally included the immediate family by blood and law, and those people who chose to live with him as relatives" (V. Deloria 109).

Dreams

1. Old Sioux was also known as Bad Hand. He had played an important role in *The Sun Dance Opera* and was referred to as being over one hundred years then in 1913. In a letter to Arthur Parker, President of the Society of American Indians, dated Dec. 14, 1916, Bonnin states: "The Old Sioux Indian, whom I've befriended for the past fourteen years is no more." See Hanson, *Sun Dance Land*.

Ballad

1. Aurora is the Roman goddess who brings dawn in her chariot.

The Indian's Awakening

1. The river of forgetfulness in Greek mythology.

2. Red River of the North runs through traditional Dakota lands and marks the boundary between North Dakota and Minnesota.

A Sioux Woman's Love for Her Grandchild

1. John 15:13.

The Sun Dance Opera

1. Shohones lived to the west of the Sioux Nation in what is now Wyoming and Idaho. Their language is Uto-Aztecan. They also practice the Sun Dance. The arrival of a stranger tests the virtue and hospitality of the host.

2. Ohiya's vow: "At the point here I stand, shawl waving. Come to me now" (trans. Deb Peterson [Mdewakanton] and Carrie Schommer [Mdewakanton]).

3. The Gossips provide trickster-like comic commentary.

4. Hebo is a *heyoka,* or contrary, doing the opposite of what is expected. In Hebo's entrance he is mistaken for a female. "Most of the so-called contrary behavior resulted from strange requirements imposed on individuals by the Thunders in a dream or a vision. Basically the idea was that if the individuals were going to receive special powers, the spirits required them to set themselves apart from the rest of the people by engaging in strange behavior that was far enough from the norm to be noticed and to be a burden to the individual" (V. Deloria 186–87).

5. Speaking to a mother-in-law was taboo in many Plains kinship structures (Lowie 82).

6. Spider was one of the incarnations of the trickster, Iktomi. Hence, to kill a spider would be to kill Iktomi. Many taboos had divine origins (Lowie 29).

7. The preceding passage demonstrates a number of cultural/social behaviors. Hebo begins by telling a joke at Sweet Singer's expense. The method of hunting buffalo is incorporated into the song. Offended, Sweet Singer breaks the social taboo that Hebo explains by passing in front of him. Not only is Sweet Singer malicious, he is also socially inept.

8. The Crier calls the participants to prayer.

9. The significance of the circle, or sacred hoop, is perhaps best explained in Neihardt's *Black Elk Speaks*: "Then I was standing on the highest mountain of them all, and round about beneath me was the whole hoop of the world. And while I stood there I saw more than I can tell and I understood more than I saw; for I was seeing in a sacred manner the shapes of all things in the spirit, and the shape of all shapes as they must live together like one being. And I saw that the sacred hoop of my people was one of many hoops that made one circle, wide as daylight and as star light, and in the center grew one mighty flowering tree to shelter all the children of one mother and one father. And I saw that it was holy" (43). The Sun Dance is performed around a circle with a sacred tree at the center.

   The Red Pipestone Quarry was "a holy place and [the Sioux] came to it often to mine the special stone they used to make Sacred Pipes," reenacting the story of the gift of the Sacred Pipe (Hoover 25).

10. *Schenawv* is the Ute language word for The Great Spirit.

11. Sarah E. Olden's description:

    A booth or shelter was [put together] near the large tipi in the center of the Circle. . . . Young men cut the tallest tree they could find for a pole and carried it along swinging between horses. In the middle of the booth they dug a deep hole in which was placed a woman's workbag containing needles, scissors, beads, and porcupine quills, together with some buffalo fat. The pole was then set up and the hole filled in. From the top of the pole was hung a cross made of green leaves to which was tied another workbag. These two bags signified liberty and freedom for the women at this special time. In fact, the pole thus erected in the early morning was properly called a "liberty pole." (V. Deloria 196)

12. "Young males gained status within their group under a strict set of guidelines. The practice of counts coups (or 'blows') among the tribes of the Great Plains supports this

idea in many ways. Coups were war honors that empha-
sized bravery, cunning, and stealth over the actual killing
of an enemy" (Holm 667).

13. The flutes accompany singing in Olden's narrative. In a
Brule Sioux story told by Henry Crow Dog, the flute is used
as a courting instrument (Erdoes and Ortiz 275–78).

14. Bonnin or Hanson may be describing a spirit entity without defaulting to "spirit."

15. I found no references to the Sun Dance and witches.

16. Dancing.

Bibliography

Albers, Patricia, and Beatrice Medicine. *The Hidden Half: Studies of Plains Indian Women*. Lanham MD: UP of America, 1983.

Bettelyoun, Susan Bordeaux, and Josephine Waggoner. *With My Own Eyes: A Lakota Woman Tells Her People's History*. Ed. Emily Levine. Lincoln: U of Nebraska P, 1998.

Biolsi, Thomas. *Organizing the Lakota: The Political Economy of the New Deal on the Pine Ridge and Rosebud Reservations*. Tucson: U of Arizona P, 1992.

Coleman, Michael C. *American Indian Children at School, 1850–1930*. Jackson: U of Mississippi P, 1993.

Deloria, Ella. *Dakota Texts*. New York: AMS Press, 1974.

Deloria, Vine, Jr. *Singing for a Spirit: A Portrait of the Dakota Sioux*. Santa Fe NM: Clear Light, 1999.

DeMallie, Raymond J., and Douglas R. Parks. *Sioux Indian Religion: Tradition and Innovation*. Norman: U of Oklahoma P, 1987.

Earlham College Archives. Gertrude Simmons Alumni File, Alumni Collection.

Eastman, Charles A. *Indian Boyhood*. Introduction by David Reed Miller. Boston: Little, Brown, 1902; Lincoln: U of Nebraska P, 1991.

Erdoes, Richard, and Alfonso Ortiz. *American Indian Myths and Legends*. New York: Pantheon, 1984.

Bibliography

Fey, Harold E., and D'Arcy McNickle. *Indians and Other Americans*. New York: Harper, 1970.

Gill, Sam D., and Irene F. Sullivan. *Dictionary of Native American Mythology*. Santa Barbara CA: ABC-CLIO, 1992.

Hanson, William F. *Sun Dance Land*. Provo: J. Grant Stevenson, 1967.

Hertzberg, Hazel W. *The Search for an American Indian Identity: Modern Pan-Indian Movements*. Syracuse NY: Syracuse UP, 1971.

Holm, Tom. "Warriors and Warfare." *Encyclopedia of North American Indians*. Ed. Frederick E. Hoxie. Boston: Houghton, 1996. 666–68.

Hoover, Herbert. *Indians of North America: The Yankton Sioux*. In collaboration with Leonard R. Bruguier. Ed. Frank W. Porter, III. New York: Chelsea, 1988.

Hoxie, Frederick E. *A Final Promise: The Campaign to Assimilate the Indians, 1880–1920*. New York: Cambridge UP, 1989.

Iverson, Peter. *Carlos Montezuma and the Changing World of American Indians*. Albuquerque: U of New Mexico P, 1982.

Jahner, Elaine. "Stone Boy: Persistent Hero." *Smoothing the Ground: Essays on Native American Oral Literature*. Ed. Brian Swann. Berkeley: U of California P, 1983. 171–86.

Kvasnicka, Robert M., and Herman J. Viola. *The Commissioners of Indian Affairs, 1824–1977*. Lincoln: U of Nebraska P, 1979.

Lone Hill, Karen D. "Sioux." *Encyclopedia of North American Indians*. Ed. Frederick E. Hoxie. Boston: Houghton, 1996. 590–93.

Lowie, Robert H. *Indians of the Plains*. Preface by Raymond J. DeMallie. New York: McGraw, 1954; Lincoln: U of Nebraska P, 1982.

Mihesuah, Devon A. *Natives and Academics: Researching and Writing about American Indians*. Lincoln, U of Nebraska P, 1998.

Montezuma Letters. Carlos Montezuma Papers. Division of Archives and Manuscripts, State Historical Society of Wisconsin.

Neihardt, John G. *Black Elk Speaks*. Introduction by Vine Deloria, Jr. New York: Morrow, 1932; Lincoln: U of Nebraska P, 1988.

Philp, Kenneth R. *John Collier's Crusade for Indian Reform, 1920–1954*. Tucson: U of Arizona P, 1977.

Prucha, Francis Paul. *The Churches and the Indian Schools, 1888–1912*. Lincoln: U of Nebraska P, 1979.

Rice, Julian. *Deer Women and Elk Men: The Lakota Narratives of Ella Deloria*. Albuquerque: U of New Mexico P, 1992.

———. *Ella Deloria's The Buffalo People*. Albuquerque: U of New Mexico P, 1994.

———. *Ella Deloria's Iron Hawk*. Albuquerque: U of New Mexico P, 1993.

Riggs, Stephen Return. *A Dakota-English Dictionary*. Washington DC: Smithsonian Institution, 1852; Minneapolis: Ross, 1968.

Stewart, Omer C. *Peyote Religion*. Norman: U of Oklahoma P, 1987.

Stout, Mary. "Zitkala-Ša: The Literature of Politics." *Coyote Was Here: Essays on Contemporary Native American Literary and Political Mobilization*. Ed. Bo Scholer. Aarhus, Denmark: SEKLOS, 1984. 70–78.

Utley, Robert M. *The Indian Frontier of the American West, 1846–1890*. Albuquerque: U of New Mexico P, 1984.

Bibliography

Walker, James R. *Lakota Belief and Ritual*. Ed. Raymond J. DeMallie and Elaine A. Jahner. Lincoln: U of Nebraska P, 1980.

————. *Lakota Society*. Ed. Raymond J. DeMallie. Lincoln: U of Nebraska P, 1982.

Warrior, Robert Allen. *Tribal Secrets: Recovering American Indian Intellectual Traditions*. Minneapolis: U of Minnesota P, 1995.

Wunder, John R. *"Retained by the People": A History of American Indians and the Bill of Rights*. New York: Oxford UP, 1994.

Zitkala-Ša (Gertrude Bonnin). *American Indian Stories*. Washington DC: Hayworth, 1921; Lincoln: U of Nebraska P, 1985.

————. *Americanize the First American: A Plan of Regeneration*. Pamphlet. 1921.

————. *Old Indian Legends*. Boston: Ginn, 1901; Lincoln: U of Nebraska P, 1985.

Writings on Zitkala-Ša

Zitkala-Ša was virtually unknown for many decades. Today she is assessed by historians and literary critics who seem to be working independently in their own disciplines. Her biographical achievements were noted in early works like Marion Gridley's *Indians of Today* (1936) and *American Indian Women* (1974), and Louis Thomas Jones's *Aboriginal American Oratory* (1965). Alice Poindexter Fisher (Dexter Fisher) broke ground with her dissertation and comparative study of Zitkala-Ša and Mourning Dove. On the cusp of multicultural studies and feminist criticism, Fisher's articles laid the groundwork for contemporary examinations of Zitkala-Ša. Fisher combined biographical review with a discussion of cultural influences and conflicts. Her *American Indian Quarterly* article was later adapted as the foreword to a reprinting of Zitkala-Ša's *American Indian Stories* (1985). Fisher's essay became an important source for many subsequent studies, despite occasional errors, particularly in regard to *The Sun Dance Opera*. Also important but often overlooked, Agnes M. Picotte's foreword to a reprinting of *Old Indian Legends* provides details and information from an indigenous point of view.

As Zitkala-Ša's work has gained interest from scholars, Mary Stout provides some basic information in her useful bibliography that complements a brief essay. In the context of "new Indian history," Alison Bernstein considers the role of Zitkala-Ša, Ella Deloria, and Ruth Muskrat Bronson (Cherokee) in the Indian New Deal. Directed by Peter Iverson, biographer of Carlos Montezuma, Debra Welch's unpublished dissertation takes a more comprehensive biographical approach. In the context of American Indian women's biographies, Laurie Lisa's

1996 dissertation, directed by Gretchen Bataille and Kathleen Sands, draws on archival materials for literary analysis. David L. Johnson and Raymond Wilson also present a biographical summary, but the article has many factual errors and little critical context. Michael Coleman discusses Bonnin's experiences in a historical examination of Indian boarding schools. Margaret Lukens's biographical essay is thorough and thoughtful in its analysis.

With postcolonial and feminist theories as foundation, many scholars have begun to reexamine Zitkala-Ša's rhetorical positioning. In some essays, however, her text is subordinated to a theoretical premise with insufficient regard to tribal issues of sovereignty and cultural context. Individual and cultural conflicts are polarized by the pitting of indigenous interests against European or Euroamerican ones, without the consideration of mediations or survival techniques. Assumptions are sometimes made about Bonnin's mixed heritage, an issue she herself never addressed.

These critical studies represent a general problem in American Indian studies in which mainstream analysis is sometimes misapplied to tribal literature. For example, Jeanne Smith is one of the few critics to discuss *Old Indian Legends*, yet she constantly refers to Zitkala-Ša as Lakota, not realizing the social distinctions between Lakota, Dakota, and Yankton Sioux. Mary Paniccia Carden argues about the placing of "Why I Am a Pagan" in relation to other autobiographical essays, but her primary source is an anthology, not *American Indian Stories,* wherein Zitkala-Ša renamed the essay and concluded the collection with a political manifesto. Carden is not the only critic to assess "Why I Am a Pagan" out of the context of Christian allegiances later in Bonnin's life or without regard to modifications in its republication as "The Great Spirit." Even noted biography theorist Sidonie Smith in her otherwise excellent examination defines Zitkala-Ša primarily in terms of American nationality rather than tribal nationality. However, Betty Louise Bell (Cherokee) perceives the complexities of the religious forces and tribal sovereignty in the essay, despite an incorrect citation.

Most literary critics discuss Zitkala-Ša's gender and race without considering the culturally specific expressions of gender complementarity among Plains Indians. Despite this oversight, Ruth Spack presents an interesting discussion of revolutionary women. Susan Benardin and Laura Wexler marshal powerful arguments about gendered influences on Zitkala-Ša's language. Martha J. Cutter, Diana Vanessa Holford, and Dorthea Susag investigate, along with Benardin and Carden, the language of self-representation. Patricia Okker and Elizabeth Ammons compellingly discuss Zitkala-Ša's writings in relationship to the literary canon.

Of the men who have written about Zitkala-Ša, D. K. Meisenheimer Jr., makes an unusual comparison with Sarah Orne Jewett in a study of regionalism. William Willard offers the most comprehensive and tribal discussions among the secondary literature in his articles in *Wicazo Ša Review*.

Perhaps the most significant recent writing is Doreen Rappaport's biographical reconstruction for young adult readers, *The Flight of Red Bird: The Life of Zitkala-Ša*. The volume is one of the few publications to discuss the whole of Zitkala-Ša's life. Thoroughly researched, it also contains a valuable chronology.

Among the challenges of writing about Zitkala-Ša specifically and American Indian literature in general is taking into account tribal interests, varied genres, cultural contexts, cross-disciplinary approaches, and the particulars of tribal history, language, and rhetoric. I hope that making more of Zitkala-Ša's writings available in this book will facilitate this task.

Selected Bibliography

Bell, Betty Louise. "'If This Is Paganism . . . ': Zitkala-Ša and the Devil's Language." *Native American Religious Identity: Unforgotten Gods*. Ed. Jace Weaver. Maryknoll NY: Orbis, 1998. 61–68.

Bernardin, Susan. "The Lessons of a Sentimental Education: Zitkala-Ša's Autobiographical Narratives." *Western American Literature* 32.3 (Nov. 1997): 212–38.

Bernstein, Alison. "A Mixed Record: The Political Enfranchisement of American Indian Women During the Indian New Deal." *Journal of the West* 23.3 (July 1984): 13–20.

Bloom, Harold. "Zitkala-Ša." *Native American Women Writers*. Philadelphia: Chelsea, 1998. 118–26.

Carden, Mary Paniccia. "'The Ears of the Palefaces Could Not Hear Me': Languages of Self-Representation in Zitkala-Ša's Autobiographical Essays." *Prose Studies* 20.1 (Apr. 1997): 58–76.

Coleman, Michael C. "Motivations of Indian Children at Missionary and U.S. Government Schools." *Montana: The Magazine of Western History* 40 (winter 1990): 30–45.

Cutter, Martha J. "Zitkala-Ša's Autobiographical Writings: The Problems of a Canonical Search for Language and Identity." *MELUS* 19.1 (spring 1994): 31–45.

Diana, Vanessa Holford. "'Hanging in the Heart of Chaos': Bi-Cultural Limbo, Self-(Re)presentation, and the White Audience in Zitkala-Ša's *American Indian Stories*." *Cimarron Review* 121 (Oct. 1, 1997): 154–73.

Dominguez, Susan. "Zitkala-Ša (Gertrude Simmons Bonnin), 1876-1938: (Re)discovering the Sun Dance." *American Music Research Center Journal* 5 (1995): 83–96.

Fisher, Dexter (Alice Poindexter). Foreword to *American Indian Stories* by Zitkala-Ša. Lincoln: U of Nebraska P, 1985. (Also published as "Zitkala-Ša: The Evolution of a Writer." *American Indian Quarterly* 5.3 [Aug. 1979]: 229–38.)

———. "The Transformation of Tradition: A Study of Zitkala-Ša and Mourning Dove, Two Transitional American Indian Writers." Diss., CUNY, 1979.

———. "The Transformation of Tradition: A Study of Zitkala-Ša and Mourning Dove, Two Transitional American Indian Writers." *Critical Essays on Native American Literature.* Ed. Andrew Wiget. Boston: Hall, 1985. 202–11.

———. "Zitkala-Ša: The Evolution of a Writer." *American Indian Quarterly* 5.3 (Aug. 1979): 229–38.

Gridley, Marion E. "Gertrude Simmons Bonnin: A Modern Progressive." *American Indian Women.* New York: Hawthorne, 1974. 81–87.

———. *Indians of Today.* Chicago: Indian Council Fire, 1936.

Hafen, P. Jane. "A Cultural Duet: Zitkala-Ša and *The Sun Dance Opera.*" *Great Plains Quarterly* 18.2 (spring 1998): 102–11.

———. "Zitkala-Ša: Sentimentality and Sovereignty." *Wicazo Ša Review* 12.2 (fall 1997): 31–42.

Hamm, Tom. "Side by Side: Zitkala-Ša at Earlham 1895–1897: From Campus to the Center of American Indian Activism." *The Earlhamite* (winter 1998): 20–22.

Hanson, William F. "The Lure of Tea-Man Nacup: Springtime Festival of the Utes." Master's thesis, Brigham Young U, 1937.

———. *Sun Dance Land.* Provo: J. Grant Stevenson, 1967.

Hoefel, Roseanne. "Writing, Performance, Activism: Zitkala-Ša and Pauline Johnson." *Native American Women in Literature and Culture.* Ed. Susan Castillo and Victor M. P. DaRosa. Porto, Portugal: Fernando Pessoa UP, 1997. 107–18.

Johnson, David L., and Raymond Wilson. "Gertrude Simmons Bonnin, 1876–1938: 'Americanize the First American.'" *American Indian Quarterly* 12 (winter 1988): 27–40.

Lisa, Laurie. "The Life Story of Zitkala-Ša/Gertrude Simmons Bonnin: Writing and Creating a Public Image." Diss., Arizona State U, 1996.

Lukens, Margaret A. "The American Story of Zitkala-Ša." *In Her Own Voice: Nineteenth-Century American Women Essayists.* Ed. Sherry Lee Linkon. New York: Garland, 1997. 141–55.

Meisenheimer, D. K., Jr. "Regionalist Bodies/Embodied Regions: Sarah Orne Jewett and Zitkala-Ša." *Breaking Boundaries: New Perspectives on Women's Regional Writing.* Ed. Sherrie A. Inness and Diana Royer. Iowa City: U of Iowa P, 1997. 109–23.

Okker, Patricia. "Native American Literatures and the Canon: The Case of Zitkala-Ša." *American Realism and the Canon.* Ed. Tom Quirk and Gary Scharnhorst. Newark: U of Delaware P, 1994. 87–101.

Picotte, Agnes M. Foreword to *Old Indian Legends* by Zitkala-Ša. Lincoln: U of Nebraska p, 1985. xi–xviii.

Rappaport, Doreen. *The Flight of Red Bird: The Life of Zitkala-Ša.* New York: Dial, 1997.

Ruoff, A. Lavonne Brown. "Early Native American Women Authors: Jane Johnston Schoolcraft, Sarah Winnemucca, S. Alice Callahan, E. Pauline Johnson, and Zitkala-Ša." *Nineteenth-Century American Women Writers: A Critical Reader.* Ed. Karen L. Kilcup. Malden MA: Blackwell, 1998.

Smith, Jeanne. "'A Second Tongue': The Trickster's Voice in the Works of Zitkala-Ša." *Tricksterism in Turn-of-the-Century American Literature: A Multicultural Perspective.* Ed. Elizabeth Ammons and Annette White-Parks. Hanover NH: UP of New England, 1994. 46–60.

Smith, Sidonie. "Cheesecake, Nymphs, and 'We the People': Un/National Subjects about 1900." *Prose Studies* 17.1 (Apr. 1994): 120–40.

Spack, Ruth. "Revisioning American Indian Women: Zitkala-Ša's Revolutionary *American Indian Stories*." *Legacy* 14.1 (1997): 25–43.

Stewart, Omer C. "Gertrude Simmons Bonnin." *University of South Dakota Bulletin*, News Report 87, Institute of Indian Studies, May 1981.

Stout, Mary. "Zitkala-Ša." *Handbook of Native American Literature*. Ed. Andrew Wiget. New York: Garland, 1996. 303–07.

———. "Zitkala-Ša: The Literature of Politics." *Coyote Was Here: Essays On Contemporary Native American Literary and Political Mobilization*. Ed. Bo Scholer. Aarhus, Denmark: SEKLOS, 1984. 70–78.

Susag, Dorothea M. "Zitkala-Ša (Gertrude Simmons Bonnin): A Power(full) Literary Voice." *Studies in American Indian Literatures* 5.4 (winter 1993): 3–24.

Welch, Deborah. "Zitkala-Ša: An American Indian Leader, 1876–1938." Diss., U of Wyoming, 1985.

Wexler, Laura. "Tender Violence: Literary Eavesdropping, Domestic Fiction, and Educational Reform." *The Culture of Sentiment: Race, Gender, and Sentimentality in Nineteenth-Century America*. Ed. Shirley Samuels. New York: Oxford UP, 1992. 9–38.

Willard, William. "The First Amendment, Anglo-Conformity and American Indian Religious Freedom." *Wicazo Ša* 7.1 (spring 1991): 25–42.

———. "Zitkala-Ša: A Woman Who Would Be Heard!" *Wicazo Ša* 1.1 (spring 1985): 11–16.

Young, Mary E. "Gertrude Simmons Bonnin." *Notable American Women 1607–1950*. Ed. Edward T. James, Janet Wilson James, and Paul S. Boyer. 3 vols. Cambridge: Belknap, 1971. 1:198–200.

Zitkala-Ša (Gertrude Bonnin). *American Indian Stories*. Washington DC: Hayworth, 1921; Lincoln: U of Nebraska P, 1985.

———. *Old Indian Legends*. Boston: Ginn, 1901; Lincoln: U of Nebraska P, 1985.